design for performance

timespace

1995 - 1999

Compiled by Peter Ruthven Hall and Kate Burnett

THE SOCIETY OF BRITISH THEATRE DESIGNERS
·S·B·T·D·

The Society of British Theatre
Designers is deeply grateful to all
the sponsors, from private
individuals to large organisations,
who have made this exhibition,
its catalogue and programme of
educational events possible.
Sincere thanks are due to:

Published in Great Britain by
The Society of British
Theatre Designers
47 Bermondsey Street,
London SE1 3XT

Registered Charity No. 800638

Text copyright © 1999

ISBN 0-9529309-1-9 ✓

British Library Cataloguing in
Publication Data: a catalogue
record of this book is available
from the British Library

Typography by Simon Head

Edited by Keith Allen
and Phyllida Shaw

Printed by Spider Web

Cover image: Pippa Nissen's
storyboard for *Faust*, 1997
(see page 14)

Photographs and illustrations are
by the contributing designer,
unless otherwise stated.

Information in this catalogue has
been provided by contributing
designers and is published in
good faith.

Imagination Entertainments
The Pairing Scheme
The Arts Council of England
The Baring Foundation
The Mackintosh Foundation
The John Lewis Partnership

John Bury
Dean Clough Galleries
Ann Curtis
Delstar Engineering Ltd
Howard Eaton Lighting Ltd
Lee Filters
Maltbury Ltd
PL Parsons Ltd
Samuelson Communications Ltd
Souvenir Scenic Studios
Stage Technologies Ltd
Talbot Designs Ltd
Triple E Ltd
Kimpton Walker Ltd
White Light Ltd

Thanks are also due to the
following for their inspiration,
commitment and practical help:

Carla Eve Amie, education notes;
Alison Benbow, exhibition
graphics; Howard Bird, ABTT
Executive Director; Jan Bee
Brown, design schools exhibition;
David Burrows, SBTD website;
David Cockayne, design schools
exhibition; Tara Conlan for Square
Mile Communications, Press
Officer; Jason Redgrave,
research; Sarah Smith,
Education Officer; Jenny Straker,
ABTT Administrator; Simon
Thomas-Colquhoun, Technical
Director; Colin Winslow, SBTD
website design.

Christopher Frayling, Rector and
Vice Provost, Royal College of Art;
Claire Allman, Martin Leyton and
Ray Martin at the Royal College
of Art.

Time + Space draws on the
resources and membership of the
following organisations, which
include theatre designers,
technicians and architects:

The Society of British
Theatre Designers

The Association of British
Theatre Technicians

The Association of
Lighting Designers

British Actors Equity
Association (Register of
Designers)

Patrons

John Bury OBE
Judi Dench DBE
Richard Eyre KBE
Beryl Grey DBE
Margaret Harris
Jeremy Isaacs KBE
Bruce McLean
Adrian Noble
Trevor Nunn CBE

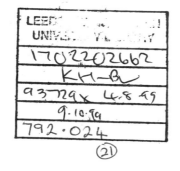

ENTERTAINMENTS

Imagination Entertainments is delighted to support Time + Space. It is both impressive and unique to see such a variety of examples of contemporary design for performance in one exhibition. I am convinced that professional and enthusiast alike will find this a fascinating exploration of how designers respond to the challenges of conveying a sense of time and space. The Society of British Theatre Designers is to be congratulated on creating this celebration of the imagination that makes British theatre the experience it is today.

Gary Withers
Creative Director

participating organisations

The Society of British Theatre Designers

The Society of British Theatre Designers (SBTD) was founded in 1971 by John Bury, with Ralph Koltai, Nicholas Georgiadis and Timothy O'Brien. It started life with the object of deciding on the most appropriate union to negotiate for designers. Since then it has developed and diversified and now has a wide membership. It aims to enhance the standing of British theatre design at home and abroad in many different ways. One of these is to organise, every four years, an exhibition of theatre design which in part represents Britain in Prague at the international Quadrennial. It also arranges seminars and forums for the discussion and development of professional practice. Designers are easily isolated by their work. Their Society puts them in touch with one another, with painters and sculptors, and with those working in theatre in other countries.

47 Bermondsey Street
London SE1 3XT
Tel: 0171 403 3778
Fax: 0171 378 6170
www.theatredesign.org.uk

The Association of British Theatre Technicians

The Association of British Theatre Technicians (ABTT) was formed in 1961 by leading exponents of the technical side of theatre. The vision was to have a network of technicians who could exchange information, advise each other of safe codes of conduct, good working practice and trade information on new technology. It was also formed to review new theatre buildings and equipment. Thirty-seven years on, the need for the Association is as great as ever. EC directives from Brussels and the Health and Safety Executive and the growth of increasingly sophisticated equipment have meant that the beleaguered technician needs as much good advice as he or she can get. The ABTT publishes codes of practice for the theatre industry, influences draft standards and regulations and offers assistance and advice to those involved in planning new or refurbishing old theatres. The Association organises an annual trade show in London and a biennial show in the north of England, in addition to members' meetings and seminars. Members of the ABTT include flymen, architects, consultants, stage managers, lighting designers, equipment suppliers, teachers, students, scenographers and production managers - in other words anyone, professional or amateur, in work or training, who has any interest in the technical aspects of theatre.

47 Bermondsey Street
London SE1 3XT
Tel: 0171 403 3778
Fax: 0171 378 6170
www.abtt.org.uk

The Association of Lighting Designers

The Association of Lighting Designers (ALD) is the professional body representing lighting designers in all fields within the United Kingdom and abroad. A voluntarily run association, it exists to provide a resource and forum for discussion and development of artistic and creative aims amongst designers from the fields of theatre, television, architecture, education, industrial and corporate presentations and manufacturing. The membership includes leading lighting designers from Britain and many other parts of the world. Corporate members enjoy access to an accurately targeted database of lighting professionals. The ALD holds regular meetings including show briefings, product demonstrations, master classes and discussion groups. It publishes a bi-monthly magazine called Focus giving details of meetings, associated events and lighting news. A directory, distributed annually to producers and other potential employers, promotes professional members of the Association. For details of how to join and the membership categories available, visit the ALD website or contact the office.

P O Box 95
Worcester Park
Surrey KT4 8XT
Tel: 0181 330 6577
Fax: 0181 330 6577
e-mail: office@ald.org.uk
www.ald.org.uk

British Actors Equity Association

Equity is delighted to be associated with the designers' exhibition at the Royal College of Art. It welcomes the opportunities afforded by this showcase of members' talent and creativity and applauds the continuing high levels of professionalism shown by designers even in the current, often difficult, financial climate. Equity currently has over 400 designers on its designers' register. It has negotiated agreements with all the major employers' groups: the Theatrical Management Association, the Society of London Theatre and the Independent Theatre Council. These agreements cover everything from billing to model expenses, from copyright to minimum fees. There is a full-time Organiser available to help with queries connected with the Equity Designers' contracts. The Organiser will also represent Designer members in the event of contractual disputes with managers. In addition, all the normal services available to members can be used by designers. Of these, the advice on tax and DSS claims provided by the Welfare Benefits Officer is particularly useful. There is also a legal service provided to members who have legal problems connected with their work. This is much used by members, especially those with personal injury problems. Equity welcomes and encourages the involvement of its designer members, and will continue to strive to maintain and improve its service to them.

Guild House
Upper St Martin's Lane
London WC2H 9EG
Tel: 0171 379 6000
Fax: 0171 379 7001
e-mail: info@equity.org.uk

contents

introduction

The intention of any production team must be to make a performance which connects with its audience. During the performance, the audience and performers are connected in their experience of time and place, both real and imaginary.

One of the most enjoyable aspects of touring Make Space! (the last Society of British Theatre Designers exhibition) to six galleries over three years, was watching visitors engage with the moments, worlds and stories presented in model boxes, drawings, photographs and artefacts. In that exhibition, categorisation of the material by different types of performance space provided the visitor with an accessible route through a huge variety of work. Four years later, we hope to have created an equally enjoyable and interesting way for viewers and readers to encounter the work of more than 140 designers, by taking as our theme space and its partner, time.

Time + Space considers how designers explore the elements of time and space in performance and as fundamental aspects of the artistic and technical production process. Designers are often asked: 'But where do you start? How did you arrive at that idea? How do you get from an idea to a design? How do you know it will work in performance? How does it work with the words, music and movement?' The questioning process is an essential part of design. Asked by a director: 'How could we put a lake on stage?' a designer might answer: 'Well, what is it about "lake-ness" that we need to convey?' Such an exchange would prompt a stream of further questions and answers, before a production decision is finally made.

Time + Space has taken some of the questions that designers ask themselves and their collaborators as 'coat hangers' for a more conversational stroll through the exhibition. We hope that this way of questioning, of batting ideas to and fro, will illuminate the images seen and the decisions designers take about how to present unfamiliar stories and themes, or re-present the familiar.

The work is organised under eight headings: Design Process; Narrative Time; Once Upon a Time: Periods Recreated; Time Transposed; Allusions to Time; Movement in Time and Space and Colour and Light in Time and Space.

These do not seek to categorise designers, who often work across many different areas of performance. Rather, the selection asks: 'How do we present this material so that it is relevant to us and our audience now, in this time, in this place?' The separate section on Colour and Light in Time and Space in no way negates the wonderful colour work in every other section, but is intended to draw attention to lighting, projection and time-based media as increasingly influential and inspiring elements of design.

We hope these questions will engage you in conversation with the images, ideas, techniques and skills presented. Some of the images stand alone. They may be arresting in colour and composition, atmospheric or evocative of space or structures which invite the viewer into a world. They may take the eye around a progression of ideas, or invite direct engagement with a character or period. Very often though, the accompanying text illuminates a second inspection of the image, indicating more of the designer's intentions than the image alone. This reminds us that the visual language of performance is a vehicle, a means, not an end in itself.

One of the most satisfying and at the same time tantalising aspects of theatre design is its ephemerality. It is always a collaboration, always about something. It is not finite, but binds together and presents other disciplines in performance. It relies upon and sometimes revels in technology. No production has the same problems to solve and each new project leads the designer to research unfamiliar territory. Theatre design is a continuing education. It is also essentially practical and pragmatic: each physical aspect of a design is measurable and capable of being assessed. Poised between art and industry, it is a discipline in a constant state of evolution, as is evident from the work you are about to see.

**Kate Burnett and
Peter Ruthven Hall**

design process

The work in this section demonstrates something of the variety of approaches to designing for performance. The process of investigation and research by the designer, alone or within a company or larger community, creates a visual arts context for the project. Time and space are the practical and technical dimensions in which designers work. What kind of space does the design occupy or create? How long is the design period and the production 'build time'? What is the technical schedule in the performance space and what are the design logistics of touring productions? These criteria all influence the artistic process.

Process also describes the exploration involved in devising a show and experimenting in different disciplines. Design here can have two almost separate elements: first, the employment of art as an expressive language for developing the dramatic material; second, the development of a design, which may be the sum of many individuals' skills and experiments, organised and sometimes transformed by the designer into a practical working vehicle.

Tom Phillips

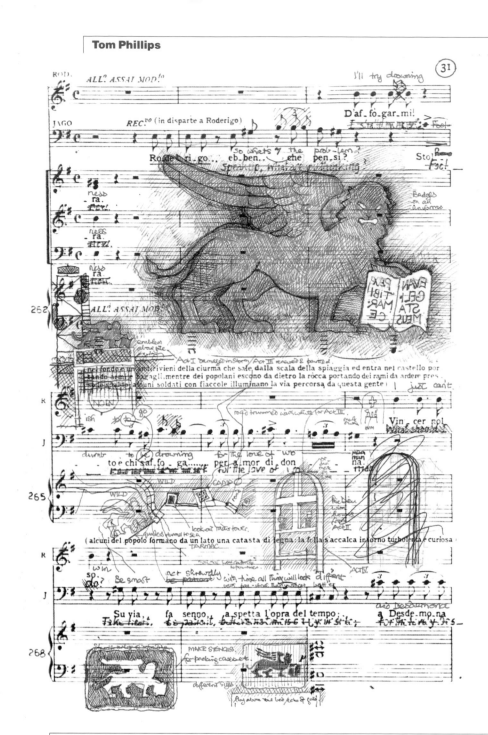

English National Opera
The London Coliseum
September 1998

Left: Studies for design, with translation

Tom Phillips: 'A visit to Famagusta, the site of the original action of *Otello*, where Otello's castle stands next to an up-to-date military camp, made a short circuit of the centuries between the two constructions. "Now" was always present as I looked at "then" and it became more relevant. I was also working on the translation where time in language allows "now" to strip away the obfuscations of "then". The two processes of designing and making the text became acts of translation in time.'

Director: David Freeman
Designer: Tom Phillips
Lighting Designer: Richard Riddell

Prologue / Anthea Haddow

Theatre Cryptic and The Shamans
Stranmillis College Theatre, Belfast
Festival at Queen's
November 1998

Right: Singer and dancer meet in dream

Lucinda Meredith: 'The design was developed through explorative workshops over one year, using collaborative techniques. These included introducing drawings, models, discussion, maquettes, garments and props into the rehearsal period as well as design games into the process. By doing so, an integrated design evolved.

Following feedback, observation of workshops and game play I was able to introduce new designs throughout the year, discarding and developing the original ideas. The design became integral to the staging, characterisation and dynamics of the production, with all areas having grown together throughout the year and become truly interdependent.'

Choreographer: Eva Magyar
Designer: Lucinda Meredith
Lighting Designer: Paul Sorley
Photographer: Renzo Mazzolini

Lucinda Meredith

Remembering Eden / Cheryl Martin and Bill Connor

BBC Philharmonic Orchestra Education Department
Studio A, BBC North - Manchester
November 1995

Kate Burnett: 'Remembering Eden was a year-long community opera project culminating in four performances featuring 70 members of the BBC Philharmonic Orchestra. Art workshops contributed both to the production design and to the devising process alongside music, movement, drama and poetry work.

'Set in Manchester, themes included medical research, animal rights protests, football, club culture, street people and true love. Clear, fire-retardant plastics, medical X-rays, pavement-type drawings and a rain curtain made up a traverse set; rain at one end, the Philharmonic at the other. The audience was raised above a "street" underworld on two banks of arena seating. Their height obviated sightline problems and made visible the choreography of so many performers. The opera's fluid movement through streets, hospital

wards, laboratories, factories, clubs and a football pitch called for almost continuous transformations. These were achieved with choreographed use of a few props and a great variety of lighting colours and effects.

Lighting designer, Ken Coker contributed many visual images during the devising process, including the football stadium curve mounted with red and green plastic par-cans. He used moving lights for maximum flexibility within very limited technical time in the performance space.'

Director: Michael Fox
Set Designer: Kate Burnett
Costume Designer: Brian Moorhouse
Lighting Designer: Ken Coker
Choreographer: Carlton 'Jackie' Guy
Conductor: Bill Connor

Kandis Cook

A Mad World My Masters'
Shakespeares Globe
1998
K. Cook

A Mad World, My Masters / Thomas Middleton

Shakespeare's Globe Theatre - London
August 1998

Left: Harebrain

Kandis Cook: 'The play is set in a moneyed period where affluence was gained through cheating one another and taking advantage of the opportunities presented by the exotic 'new worlds'. It describes the categories in which the women found themselves or in which they chose to remain. The fear of women and the inadequacy of the male characters in understanding and equalling them, created the dichotomy and dynamics of the production. We decided to connect this period to the kick and scramble of the last 30 years of the 20th century, where window dressing a personality and the disguise of truth lead us back to the gulling of a mad world (See also page 66).

Director: Sue Lefton
Designer: Kandis Cook
Music: Claire Van Kampen
Photographer: Chris Moyse

Newport Arts Centre
Newport, Wales
1999

Right: Configurations of the studio theatre

Frank Woods: 'Newport County Borough Council was awarded a grant from the Arts Council of Wales to develop designs for a new arts centre to be sited on the banks of the River Usk, near the town centre.

'The theatre and studio theatre are being designed for companies on the middle and small-scale professional circuits and for an educational and community arts programme. Music, dance, comedy and film will be featured in both.

'Though the main stage is traditional in format, the seating is asymmetric in layout, on two raked tiers, which are linked on one side. This increases the cohesion of the audience, provides some premium seats and minimises the loss of atmosphere when only small numbers are present. The studio theatre offers flexibility in layout. The dance studio and recording studio are community facilities, open to amateurs and professionals. Workshops and studio facilities will be provided for arts and crafts activity.'

Architects: Austin-Smith:Lord
Theatre Consultants: Carr and Angier

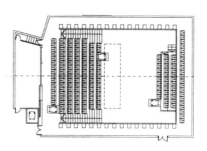

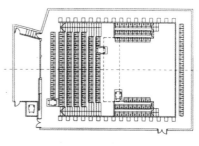

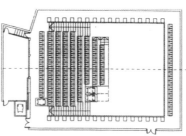

Chris Dyer

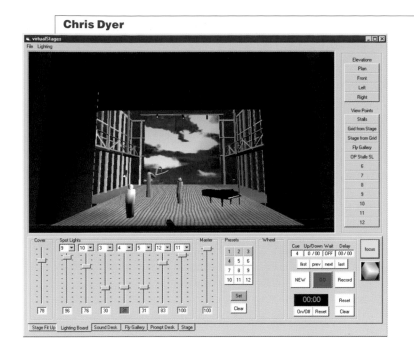

Virtual Stages
Research Project
Central Saint Martin's College of
Art and Design - London

Screen grab of the interface of *Virtual Stages* showing a model for *Un Re in Ascolto* at the Royal Opera House.

Chris Dyer: '*Virtual Stages* is a research project that I am directing at Central Saint Martin's College of Art and Design. It is an attempt to update the model box and at the same time give the production team a more powerful tool with which to visualise their production. It puts the systems of theatre - lights, sound, flies, trucks, revolves etc. - into a 3D computer model of a theatre. By attaching scenic elements to these systems it is possible to have a virtual technical rehearsal, which is run from a simulated prompt desk and includes light and sound cues.'

Frank Woods

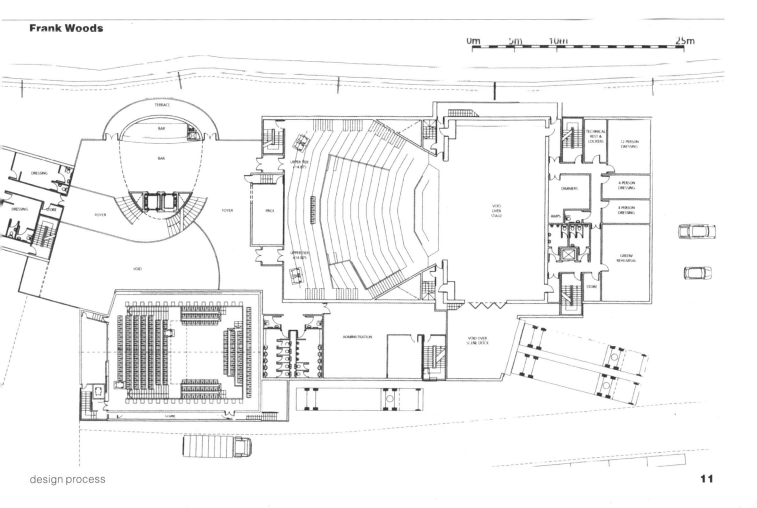

design process

Anthony Lamble

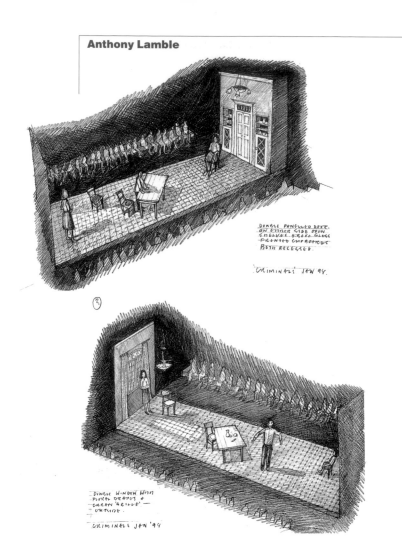

double panelled door. on either side open shelves plate glass fronted cupboards. both recessed.

CRIMINALS JAN 94.

(3)

double window with pencil drapes & chain 'grille' outside.

CRIMINALS JAN '94

The Criminals / José Triana, adapted by Adrian Mitchell

Backchat Theatre Company at the Lyric Studio, Hammersmith - London
March 1998

Left: A room, a table, three chairs, rolled up carpets, dirty curtains with large floral patterns, flower vases, a small bell, a knife and other objects, which are not used. Time: the 1960s.

Anthony Lamble: 'These two sketches represent an exploration of the play in the traverse shape. They describe episodes from a piece that was only previously produced in an end-on scenario. It also gave us an opportunity to look at the relationship between the main scenic components (i.e. window, door and shelves) their shape, position and character. The director and I worked very closely during the early stages of our collaboration. The 2D format enabled me to use the fax machine to involve him fully in the design process, despite the fact that one of us was based in Leeds and the other in London.'

Director: Ian Brown
Designer: Anthony Lamble
Lighting Designer: Kevin Sleep

Chris Victory

The Hippolytos / David Lan

Theatre Mélange
Touring
February 1998

Left: Hippolytos' death

Chris Victory: 'Working with Mélange presented a different set of problems from usual. As an ensemble company, devising the production and for a tour meant that the design developed as the rehearsals developed. Fluidity was the key to the design, with a core of eight to ten actors assuming many transformations during the piece. Essentially the play began with all the actors as a chorus from which the action evolved. Correspondingly, a basic chorus costume was added to with the use of varying weights of fabric shawls and wraps. The set was a simple floorcloth and backdrop upon which I played with light and colour.'

Director: Sandy Maberley
Designer and Lighting: Chris Victory
Choreographer: Tom Wu
Photographer: Philip Carr

Scary Antics / Devised by the group

Shysters Theatre Company
Belgrade Studio - Coventry
June 1998

Nettie Edwards / Michael E Hall:
'A young woman's freefall into self-
discovery - *Alice in Wonderland* meets
Trainspotting. Ten actors inhabit a world
where time and space are mutable. The
stage is both theatre and psyche. Utilising
music, text, mask work, mime and lighting
and exploring storytelling in a defiantly
non-naturalistic way, this piece was a
further example of the challenging and
provocative work currently being devised
and produced by companies of actors
with learning difficulties.'

Director: Richard Hayhow
Designer: Nettie Edwards
Lighting Designer: Michael E Hall
Text: Alex Jones
Movement: Rachel Karafistan

Faust / Mark Ravenhill

Actors Touring Company
Lyric Studio, Hammersmith - London and touring
February 1997

Above: A scene from the storyboard

Pippa Nissen: 'The development of the design
of *Faust* happened concurrently with the writing
of the script, the making of a video for the
performance and the initial rehearsal period.
Scenes were made by suggesting an edge to an
implied space or by using video to represent a
place naturalistically. The elements of the set
became the other members of the cast and the
real journey of the narrative is mirrored by the
dance that the set plays around the characters;
in the moving screens, the sliding panel, the
television set, and the iron bed.'

See also front cover image

Director: Nick Philippou
Designer: Pippa Nissen
Lighting Designer: Zerlina Hughes
Music: Neil Stare
Video: Alain Pelletier

narrative time

Narrative Time is the sequence or unfolding of events. A basic human faculty or instinct is to make patterns or meaning out of experience. The designer aims to create a meaningful progression of images, using juxtaposition, proportion, scale and colour, as well as information on character, status, period and location. Sometimes the set remains sculpturally the same, while lighting, costumes and props reclothe it or alter within it. Sometimes changes in location or time are marked by physical changes to the set. The nature of these changes indicates the style of the production, or they may be a product of it. They can tell the audience whose story is being unfolded and by whom. Are the changes to the characters and their environment made by the characters themselves? Are the performers the storytellers or the presenters of their material. The storyboard has become a vital tool of costume, set and lighting designers, for working out and presenting the visual progression of the production. It can indicate the balance and pattern of the whole production, while marking the significance of specific changes. Computerised simulation seeks to address these aspects, amongst others, but it is the layout of the entire progression of a narrative which demonstrates the relationship of the parts to the whole.

Dawn Allsopp

The Importance of Being Earnest
Oscar Wilde

Swan Theatre - Worcester
September 1998

Left: Act 1
Below left: Act 3

Dawn Allsopp: 'Having researched the social etiquette of the 1890s we decided that Wilde's characters were trapped inside a fragile glass environment of their own making, acting out a grotesque game of manners. Within this the design had to transform into three distinct settings whilst maintaining a stylish coherence. An exaggerated and raked chessboard floor became our visual metaphor, surrounded by painted Perspex screens. These were seemingly suggestive of papered walls in Algernon's flat (Act 1), an avenue of trees in the garden (Act 2) and steamy glass in the conservatory of Manor House (Act 3).'

Director: Jenny Stephens
Designer: Dawn Allsopp
Lighting Designer: Nick Marston

Elroy Ashmore

A Little Night Music / Stephen Sondheim

Theatre Royal - Plymouth
April 1995

Shadowlands / William Nicholson

Haymarket Theatre - Basingstoke
April 1996

Elroy Ashmore: 'With its classical columns and Latin script, the set establishes the male enclave of academic Oxford in the 1950s. This design becomes the ivory tower into which the poet Joy Davidman enters CS Lewis's life. Trees penetrate the set, but they are only barren and wintry. However there is another time-space, the world of Narnia which breaks through with the use of sliding panels and magical lighting. Glimpses of that other world are briefly exposed. Lighting plays an important role in this production and as the play progresses, the set warms through from outside; the translucent panels finally glowing in golden sunlight.'

Director: Hugh Wooldridge
Designer: Elroy Ashmore
Lighting Designer: Hugh Wooldridge

Martyn Bainbridge: 'A Little Night Music's moment in time is a weekend in the country at the turn of the century. On one level it portrays its characters in a romanticised setting, posturing on a theme of love. On another level it is a timeless dissection of relationships and marital infidelities. Weaving throughout the piece is an erotic dreamworld with its characters trapped in a "dance to the music of time". I have attempted to synthesise these elements in the stylised setting.'

Director: Roger Redfarn
Set Designer: Martyn Bainbridge
Costume Designer: Bill Butler
Lighting Designer: Mark Henderson

Keith Baker

Night Must Fall / Emlyn Williams

Swan Theatre - Worcester
October 1997

Left: Olivia confronts Danny

Keith Baker: 'Breaking with tradition, Emlyn Williams' psychological thriller is told as a flashback, effectively eliminating the "whodunit" element. The gauze walls dissolve to reveal rooms beyond, which themselves melt to show the gallows-like forest surrounding the bungalow. The characters inhabit a claustrophobic world in which eavesdropping and gossip are the main occupations, until a headless corpse is found in the garden. The ceiling panel/moon was used to display slides of the murdered woman, always watching her killer as he stalks his next victim. We were keen to present the terrifying world of Hitchcock and the German Expressionists, rather than a cosy thriller.'

Director: Jenny Stephens
Designer: Keith Baker
Lighting Designer: Nick Marston

Keith Baker

Who's Afraid of Virginia Woolf
Edward Albee

Swan Theatre - Worcester
October 1998

Left: End of Act 3

Keith Baker: 'Set in 1962, Albee's play encompasses both domestic and national themes. The American flag has been abstracted into the setting; clashing red and white walls fractured by decades of violence, against a stylised, starry sky. The circular Regency room hints at the White House, a boxing ring and a debating chamber and provides a link with George and Martha's historical namesakes. At the close of Act 2, the stars reveal the face of their fictional son. At the end of Act 3, the sky/flag tears open to reveal an optimistic new dawn.'

Director: Mark Babych
Designer: Keith Baker
Lighting Designer: Nick Marston

Janet Bird

Marat-Sade / Peter Weiss

Next Stage
The Great Hall, Sandfield Centre - Nottingham
March 1998

Left: The persecution and assassination of Marat, as performed by the inmates of the asylum

Janet Bird: 'The "play" is performed in a steeply tapering, tiled hall, its hard, clinical walls seeping moisture. Those selected from the population of the institution squeeze on to the stage via a single steel door; there is no escape. The "actors" are herded like sheep into the narrow confines or allowed to roam into the open spaces, all under the watchful eye of the Marquis de Sade, who conducts the action from his self-appointed throne, downstage right.'

Director: Geoff Bullen
Set Designer: Janet Bird
Costume Designer: Marilyn Bullen
Lighting Designer: Alistair Bland
Photographer: Gerald Murray

This image has been sponsored by Next Stage

David Burrows

Tartuffe / Molière

THOK
National Theatre of Cyprus - Nicosia
March 1997

Left: Act 1 The entrance hall of Orgon's house
Below left: Act 4 After dinner cigars and brandy; Marianne pleads with her father to change his mind

David Burrows: 'The housekeeper, Dorine, was the production's pivotal character. From dawn and Madame Pernelle's angry departure, to the King's Officer's fortuitous arrival and Tartuffe's arrest, the play's action revolved around her duties - dusting, hoovoring, cooking and as persistent advisor to all - on a most eventful day. The set design's aesthetic echoed the spirit of Russian constructivism and the costumes suggested the 1920s. As the action moved around Orgon's house, the locations rapidly transformed in a blue mirror-balled atmosphere, to music reflecting the play's unfolding sense of impending disaster; a ballet of stage trucks.'

Director: Alkis Kritikos
Designer: David Burrows
Lighting Designer: Gregoris Papageorgiou
Music: Barry Wickens and Brian Betts

These images have been sponsored by
Wimbledon School of Art

Lucky Sods / John Godber

Coliseum Theatre - Oldham
January 1997

Above: Act 2, scene 2 The tulip field

Rachel Blues: 'The action takes place in
eight different locations over a period of
twelve months. The design balances
simplicity with flexibility avoiding the need
for complex scene changes. The two
curved walls enabled us to manipulate the
space to suggest various interiors and
exteriors, whilst a back projection screen
with its carefully chosen palette of colour
further enhanced mood and location. In
each scene I focused on one element of
the location to give it a sense of place. So,
for example, the tulip field in Amsterdam is
created by giant tulips painted on to a
filled-in gauze.'

Director: Gareth Tudor Price
Designer: Rachel Blues
Lighting Designer: Mark Howarth

Anne Curry

The Rise and Fall of Little Voice
Jim Cartwright

New Vic Theatre - Newcastle under Lyme
May 1996

Left: Act 2: Ray, Marie, Sadie and Little Voice

Anne Curry: 'Ray, Marie and Sadie are ready to
move off to the club. The figure on the right is
Little Voice, here represented at the climax of her
vocal performance at the club. There is a
spotlight on her in a glitter dress, with a mirror
ball in the background. I often design costumes
using actor groupings, as indicated by the script,
because they will be seen this way together on
stage. It seems natural to work on them together
on one sheet of paper.'

Director: Rob Swain
Designer: Anne Curry
Lighting Designer: Paul W Jones
Musical Director: Greg Palmer

Philip Engleheart

Robin Hood / Jack Holloway and Steve Byrne

South Hill Park Arts Centre
Wilde Theatre - Bracknell
November 1997

Philip Engleheart: 'I chose real time and a big sky as the vehicle for this poetic ballad, seen through a silhouetted, derelict tithe-barn, where each setting is made using barrels, planks and trestles. The natural, close-of-day lighting describes not only the seasons of the year but those of Robin's life. It begins with spring: birth, fresh light; moves into summer: adulthood and the streaking, warm colours of dusk; then to autumn: dangerous, raging oranges, as the battles and torchings ensue, and gives over to a star-studded, moonlit winter night, augmented by twelve candles, as the Green-man cycle completes itself. Indiscernible cross-fades and sporadic snowfall lend a truly magical atmosphere to this legend.'

Director: Steve Byrne
Designer: Philip Engleheart
Lighting Designer and Photographer:
Charlotte McClelland

Jens Cole

The Thief of Lives / Roderick Stewart

Northern Stage
Newcastle Playhouse - Newcastle upon Tyne
August 1997

Left: The field of bones

Jens Cole: 'For this new writing, based on the epic Greek model, designs were developed alongside the script. As a writer, director and designer team, our approach was fluid, aiming for total physical and visual integration of the design into the action. Choreographed interludes fused visual commentary with changes of time and space; the whispering Chorus appearing to draw in light, whilst the set changes behind them. A long central axis dominated: a new central aisle for the Chorus cut through the auditorium, the forestage extended to meet it and massive rolling steel doors, upstage centre, opened to apparent infinity. Variations in scale juxtaposed the domestic and epic: natural elements and found objects, like this fallen tree from a local forest, highlighted cyclical connections between the characters and their environment.'

Director: Ed Robson
Designer: Jens Cole
Lighting Designer: Nial Black
Choreographer: Liv Lorent
Photographer: Keith Pattison

Opera Triple Bill
Der Zar lässt sich photographieren / Kurt Weill
Der Diktator / Ernst Krenek
Der Kaiser von Atlantis / Viktor Ullmann

Guildhall School of Music and Drama - London
June 1997

Top: Der Zar lässt sich photographieren
Right: Der Diktator
Below right: Der Kaiser von Atlantis

Isabella Bywater: 'This was a student production on a very small budget. We performed three short operas written before or during the second world war, with the common subject of dictators. The last opera was written in the Terezin concentration camp and the manuscript was found after the war, hidden in the camp. The composer and others preparing the opera were killed before they were able to perform it.'

Directors: Martin Lloyd-Evans / Stephen Medcalf
Designer: Isabella Bywater
Lighting Designer: Ian Sommerville
Photographer: Christopher Simon Sykes

Sophie Tyrrell

Orfeo / Claudio Monteverdi

The Barber Opera
Barber Institute of Fine Art Concert Stage -
Birmingham
October 1997

Sophie Tyrrell: 'A sky full of stars, inspired by early Renaissance Christian paintings, was created as a gauze canopy above the performers' heads. On the earth below, Orfeo celebrates his marriage. The canopy was supported on poles rising out of the orchestra pit. The pit also allowed entrances to be made from the underworld. This action was mirrored in Orfeo's climactic ascension to heaven as he climbed above the suddenly transparent sky. This provided a solution to the problem of staging the epic journey through hell, earth and heaven within the confines of a small art-deco concert hall.'

Director: John La Bouchardiere
Designer: Sophie Tyrrell
Lighting Designer: Tom Manning
Music Director: Colin Timms

Marjoke Henrichs

Our Day Out / Willy Russell

Wolsey Theatre - Ipswich
April 1998

Marjoke Henrichs: 'Twenty-four school children and their teachers are enjoying a day on a bus, visiting a variety of places, including a zoo, a castle, the beach with high cliffs and a fairground, creating total chaos at every venue. The set is timeless, but gives the feel of the entire journey. The costumes and music were set in the 1970s.'

Director: Andrew Breakwell
Designer: Marjoke Henrichs
Lighting Designer: Adam Clark
Choreographer: Jo Jelly
Musical Director: Robert Rigby

Peter Ruthven Hall

Jenufa / Leos Janacek

Royal Northern College of Music
Manchester
March 1999

Peter Ruthven Hall: 'On one level
Jenufa is a tale set in a secluded Moravian
farming community; Janacek used Czech
word rhythms to inspire his musical line.
On another level, it is a harsh
psychological drama; Jenufa's illegitimate
baby is drowned under the ice by her
foster mother in order to preserve them
from shame. We first meet Jenufa outside
the mill, in the autumn, just before her
drunken fiancé is forbidden to marry her.
Four months later, their child is born and
Jenufa is confined in a secret room; it is
now severe winter. The baby is taken away
and murdered; the Angel of Death passes
through the house. In the spring, Jenufa is
about to marry her half cousin. As the
weather warms, the ice thaws and the
baby's body is discovered. Her secret is
out. But only as her foster mother admits
her guilt and is led away, does Jenufa
finally discover true love in her betrothed.'

Director: Stefan Janski
Designer: Peter Ruthven Hall
Lighting Designer: Philip L Edwards

Robin Don

The Storm / Alexander Ostrovsky, translated by Frank McGuinness

The Almeida Theatre - London
November 1998

Robin Don: 'The play has five locations, set in a small town on the Volga (1840). The semi-circular back wall of the Almeida gives the space an instant arena quality. With the addition of a raked floor, made from crumbling planks, the acting area was denoted. Minimal additions carved a fresh dynamic into each scene: chairs and carpet made an interior; a sturdy dome effect gave us the interior of the crumbling building; ultra-violet light was used to highlight the moon on its nocturnal path around the galactic auditorium.'

Director: Hettie MacDonald
Designer: Robin Don
Lighting Designer: Peter Mumford

The Winter Guest
Sharman MacDonald

The Almeida Theatre - London and West Yorkshire Playhouse - Leeds
February 1995

Left: The beach

Robin Don: 'Sharman MacDonald carves her plays out of space, like a sculptor attacking a solid mountain of granite. She writes with a freedom that has left many a designer crying by the wayside. Since the Almeida Theatre has no fly tower or wing space, the designated landscapes needed to coexist within the same cubic area. With the director, we carved out the required areas for upstairs house interior, downstairs by the fire, on the prom, beach with snowman (real snow) and out on the frozen sea. The subtle changes of lighting allowed each scene equal importance.'

Director: Alan Rickman
Designer: Robin Don
Lighting Designer: Peter Mumford

Ken Harrison

Travels With My Aunt / Graham Greene, adapted by Giles Havergal

Pitlochry Festival Theatre
May 1996

Left: Customs in Paris
Left middle: Hotel St James
Left below: Visconti's garden

Ken Harrison: 'A piece of finely tuned narrative theatre where the role of the principal character, Henry Pulling, is shared by four actors. The design was based on a series of storyboard images where changes of location were suggested by use of projections and shapes or light, within the discrete Perspex box representing Henry's discrete world. As Henry reaches Paraguay and finds a new life, the set opens out to reveal a garden of orange bushes reaching to the back of the stage.'

Director: Richard Baron
Designer: Ken Harrison
Lighting Designer: Kevin Sleep

Jonathan Fensom

Angels and Saints / Jessica Townsend

Soho Theatre Company
Pleasance Theatre - London (Soho Season)
November 1998

Jonathan Fensom: 'Noreen washes her dying grandmother, Catriona, in the tiny bathroom of their home. Autumn leaves fall throughout the play, representing the slow intrusion of the outside world on this isolated inner sanctum and on Noreen's life.'

Director: Polly Teale
Designer: Jonathan Fensom
Lighting Designer: Jason Taylor

*This image has been sponsored by
Soho Theatre Company*

Animal Farm / George Orwell
adapted by Ian Wooldridge

Northern Stage, middle-scale tour
September 1996

Catherine Hieatt: 'Time: 1943/45, England,
Ministry of Information, publication, censorship,
peace and freedom, Russian Allies, Lenin, Stalin.

'Space: Russia, Europe, Britain, borders,
refugees, land, country, patriotism, landscape,
fields, ploughing, planting, sowing, reaping,
ownership, farmhouse, farmyard, windmill, barn,
coop, sty, stable.

'The theatrical space is an arena of mud. There is
an old bath, a piano, some pallets, rope, naked
light bulbs, a grandfather clock, a lampstand,
three chairs, suitcases, an umbrella, and the
writing on the wall. The primary intention of the
design is to strip away the fable and reveal the
allegory. The work boot and the boot of
oppression created the stamp of the animals. In
that arena of mud, the physical struggle ensued.'

Director: Alan Lyddiard
Designer: Catherine Hieatt
Lighting Designer: Peter Barlow
Choreographer: Frank McConnell
Photographer: Keith Pattison

Keith Lodwick

The Lady of the House of Love
Angela Carter, adapted by David Kirkup and Keith Lodwick

Rear Window Theatre Company at
The Bookshop, BAC - London
October 1998

Left: The Countess and the Soldier

Keith Lodwick: 'An intimate chamber piece for three vampires, set in the drawing room of a Transylvanian castle over the course of one night. The piece was conceived, from the outset, as a site-specific promenade performance. The domestic dimensions of the former bookshop at BAC were exploited and the entire space utilised by both actors and audience. The play was a dramatic discourse on the nature of darkness and illumination. The protagonists were trapped in a linear time frame that moved inexorably towards the climax of sunrise. It was essential to intensify the dramatic qualities of light and its absence within the production, in order to convey the redeeming and destructive consequences of both.'

Director: Daniel Carey
Set Designer: Keith Lodwick
Lighting Designer: Rob Pepper

Claire Lyth

The Government Inspector
Nikolai Gogol

Theatr Clwyd - Mold
March 1996

Left: Act 1, scene 1

Claire Lyth: 'The play was updated from the original, which was set in 1835, to pre - revolutionary Russia c.1912. The set was designed to underline the satirical element of the play by using exaggerated scale. The Mayor's house was represented by huge double doors overlooking first a chaotic office, awash with bribes and unfiled papers, then a drawing room in which the mayor's enormous armchair dominated the miniature furniture for lesser mortals. The final scene became an empty space - all possessions and hopes gone with the Government Inspector.'

Director: Michael Bogdanov
Designer: Claire Lyth
Lighting Designer: Nick Schlieper

Celia Perkins

A Different Way Home / Jimmy Chin

Coliseum Theatre - Oldham
February 1997

Left: Act 1: Leslie's kitchen

Celia Perkins: 'Leslie's home was a reflection of his sad, lonely existence, dominated by his mother and memories of his uneventful life. Using a simple revolve, his 60 years were contained within the two rooms, crammed with symbols of the security of a life spent with his mother. Subtle changes in the lighting gradually unsettled the audience into the realisation that Maureen's presence in the house signified the end of the home's role as a comfort and sanctuary to Leslie and a Pandora's box of bitterness and past recriminations against his sister. '

Director: Kenneth Alan Taylor
Designer: Celia Perkins
Lighting Designer: Jezz Hellins
Sound Designer: Julie Washington

Fred Meller

Skylight / David Hare

The Watermill Theatre Company
Newbury
October 1998

Fred Meller: 'Time in Skylight is a precious commodity: the characters have spent time apart and have this moment to make or break their relationship. The twelve hours before dawn provide for an emotional flashpoint where time stops. An image for the potential of people to change or remain the same. Changing artificial light sources contrasted sharply with the small window of natural light. Finally the wall of books is torn down, allowing for time's solution itself, a glorious winter sunrise of a new day penetrating the now hazardous and wrecked room.'

Director: Euan Smith
Designer: Fred Meller
Lighting Designer: Robert Bryan

This image has been sponsored by Les Dennis

The Cherry Orchard / Anton Chekhov

Method and Madness
Touring
January 1998

Peter McKintosh: 'Under the banner of 20>20
Vision the Method and Madness ensemble is
presenting five plays, performed in repertoire,
which represent the 20th century. In *The Cherry
Orchard* (1904), the first play, the company takes
a fresh look at one of Russia's greatest plays.
High spirited and full of colour, it follows ten
comic characters whose fates depend on the
survival or destruction of a beautiful orchard.'

Director: Mike Alfreds
Designer: Peter McKintosh
Lighting Designer: Chris Davey
Photographer: Manuel Harlan

The Threepenny Opera / Bertolt Brecht and Kurt Weill

Northern Stage
Newcastle Playhouse - Newcastle upon Tyne
March 1998

First Act Finale

Neil Murray: 'An army of contemporary, homeless beggars
are living in a ruined baroque opera house. In this space they
present their opera, set in Victorian England with a
"magnificence such as only beggars can imagine, and an
economy such as only beggars can afford". This photograph
fixes the moment when a traverse curtain, made of underwear
and old net curtains, is drawn behind the Peachums as they
sing the first finale. In front of them, on the floor, a misty mirror
presents a focal point where "actors" will stand to declaim the
narrations. The Peachums wear an assortment of stolen
costumes and wigs.'

Director and Designer: Neil Murray
Lighting Designer: Tina MacHugh
Choreographer: Liv Lorent
Musical Director: Alan Fearon
with members of the Northern Sinfonia
Photographer: Keith Pattison

This image has been sponsored by Northern Stage

Neil Murray

A Version of Twelfth Night
William Shakespeare, adapted by
Alan Lyddiard

Northern Stage
Newcastle Playhouse - Newcastle upon Tyne
June 1997

Neil Murray. 'By removing four rows of seats,
stripping the space bare and injecting massive
blocks of brickwork to match the auditorium, a
huge, industrial, garage-style space was
created. An "inspection pit" was filled with water
to create a pool beneath floor panels, which were
raised and lowered with motorised chain
winches. Into this space a group of Polish artists
arrive by van to perform their version of *Twelfth
Night*. Being romantically inclined, heavy
drinkers, they have with them 200 empty Vodka
bottles and 200 red roses with which they create
a constantly changing installation during the
performance.'

Director: Alan Lyddiard
Designer: Neil Murray
Lighting Designer: Jeanine Davies
Musical Director: Iain Johnstone
Photographer: Keith Pattison

*This image has been sponsored
by Northern Stage*

What the Butler Saw / Joe Orton

Crucible Theatre - Sheffield
September 1997

Christopher Oram: 'The basic set remains unchanged throughout the production, whilst the characters run progressively out of control, swapping identities and their clothes (deliberately bold against the clinically white space) until the final few minutes. Suddenly bathed in red light, the doors are barred and, to the accompaniment of a Malcolm Arnold march, a vast metal ladder is thrust into the centre of the set to release them into the world outside. During the course of the action the characters are constantly changing their identities by swapping clothes with one another; each costume therefore has a strong individual colour in order to simplify the journey of the character until they are finally naked and order is restored.'

Director: Michael Grandage
Designer: Christopher Oram
Lighting Designer: Jeanine Davies
Photographer: Simon Warner

*These images have been sponsored
by Sheffield Theatres*

Janet Vaughan

Echoes & Omens
Devised by the company and scripted by
Carran Waterfield

Bare Essentials Youth Theatre
May 1998

Janet Vaughan: 'Echoes & Omens was
devised by young people in response to
images of the holocaust received through
films like Schindler's List. A stark and
challenging work, it crudely pitted the
cruel and powerful school bully Germans
against their target Jews, reflecting, in a
distorted way, something of the group
dynamic. All in Hitler Youth-style gym kits,
the "Jews" wore an identifying item
strapped across their backs. The older
girls played the Germans, glamorous with
their icy blue feather boas, and sat on
silver umpires' chairs. Physically raised
above the rest, they controlled them with
interrogation spotlights. Plastic gloves,
filled with blood, hung above the stage.'

Director: Richard Talbot
Design and Lighting: Janet Vaughan

The Merchant of Venice
William Shakespeare

Royal Lyceum Theatre - Edinburgh
Touring
October 1996

Left: Shylock's House

Sarah Williamson: 'The brief was to create the
illusion of travelling between many different
places in little or no real time. The set was made
up of sixteen flown painted gauzes of various
shapes and sizes, the choreography of which
allowed for quick, smooth and silent
transformations. This was helped by the ability to
bleed through - or block out - the gauzes with
light, revealing or concealing people and places
in a matter of seconds. The few architectural
structures were skeletal and also covered with
gauze, adding to the sense of a liquid space in
which nothing is solid or dependable.'

Director: Kenny Ireland
Designer: Sarah Williamson
Lighting Designer: Andy Phillips

Boris Godunov
Modest Petrovich Musorgsky

English National Opera
The London Coliseum
November 1998

Hildegard Bechtler: 'A tormented Boris
(John Tomlinson) asks the Simpleton
(Timothy Robinson) to pray for him. He
replies that he cannot pray for a "Tsar
Herod". The people are about to push the
wall, against which they are seen leaning,
in a violent scene change, propelling the
action towards Boris's meeting with the
Boyars and his death.'

Director: Francesca Zambello
Set Designer: Hildegard Bechtler
Costume Designer: Nicky Gillibrand
Lighting Designer: Wolfgang Göbbel
Choreographer: Deni Sayers
Photographer: William Rafferty

Tom Piper

Andrea Chénier / Umberto Giordano

Norwegian National Opera - Oslo
October 1999

Ian Sommerville: 'Andrea Chénier is set at the height of the French Revolution but is typical verismo opera, glorifying in the themes of love and death and human suffering against a background of turbulent times. For the second act, the composer had in mind one set, but this design reflects the episodic nature of the music. In this brief moment, the reigning revolutionaries are greeted by the populace. The blade over their heads reminds us that they have only days before they share the same fate of the many thousands at the guillotine.'

Directors: Vernon Mound and
Anthoula Papadakis
Set and Lighting Designer: Ian Sommerville
Costume Designer: Katherine Hysing
Choreographer: Anthoula Papadakis

Measure for Measure / William Shakespeare

Royal Shakespeare Company
Royal Shakespeare Theatre - Stratford-upon-Avon
April 1998

Tom Piper. 'We are inside a tower of white wood - Angelo's monument to purity - with his staircase to heaven. However, beneath the surface the true nature of his government will be revealed. The floor had traps and a spiral staircase descending to the prison below. I wanted the feeling that with each scene we were deeper within the tower. Only with the acts of compassion in the final act could we escape: a series of plank-width windows lining the stairs opened up to create lit niches, thereby breaking the formality of the set and allowing the world to breathe.'

Director: Michael Boyd
Designer: Tom Piper
Lighting Designer: Heather Carson
Photographer: Bob Collier

This image has been sponsored by the Royal Shakespeare Company

Adrian Vaux

Alma / Joshua Sobol

Cameri at Zoa House - Tel Aviv,
Israel
December 1998

Adrian Vaux: 'The play explores
the life and loves of Alma Schindler,
her marriage to Gustav Mahler, her
relationships with Gropius and
Kokoshka, and her marriage to
Franz Werfal. The set attempts to
suggest the eroticism,
claustrophobia and the ephemeral
nature of love and collected
reminders of joy, pain, music and
life; a mobile junk shop of
memorabilia. The play was first
performed in Vienna in 1996, in the
restored Secessionist Hoffmann
Purkersdorf Sanitorium and was
directed by Paulus Manker. That
version lasted more than nine hours
and the audience was invited to
choose a route through the play on
three separate evenings,
journeying through a complex
space in the spirit of celebration.
These images show two settings
from a shortened version,
condensed into one evening and
directed by the author.'

Director: Joshua Sobol
Set Designer: Adrian Vaux
Costume Designer: Edna Sobol
Lighting Designer: Felice Ross

Jamie Vartan

Tho Hansel Gretel Machine

Part one of the Lost Child Trilogy / Devised by the company

David Glass Ensemble
UK and overseas tour
1998

Jamie Vartan: 'The opening family tableau shows the moments before Gretel's birth. There is a strong sense of waiting, time passing, foreboding, life hanging by a thread. Each character occupies his or her own space, but still within the same frame. The father sits at 90 degrees to the floor, drinking soup, while Hansel makes his way slowly down a ladder. It is, as with every image in the production, resonant of a child's vision, where the illogical inner world of the imagination makes sense.'

Director and Lighting Designer: David Glass
Designer: Jamie Vartan
Photographer: Laurie Lewis

Michael Spencer

The Three Sisters / Anton Chekhov, adapted by David Mamet

Harrogate Theatre
April 1997

Michael Spencer: 'All of Chekhov's plays deal with time - the absurd waste of it. This was the third Mamet Chekhov on which Andrew Manley and I collaborated. At our first meeting I said: "It's all about people going round in circles all their lives - going nowhere," and then, almost as a joke: "Maybe they could go round on a revolve throughout the performance?" Andrew liked this. It made sense. The revolve moved almost imperceptibly - one revolution every 30 minutes. The actors sat in limbo in a vast waiting room before "going on". The revolve settings and furniture were purely functional, apart from the arch, which made us conscious of time passing and provided a constantly changing, framed tableau.'

Director: Andrew Manley
Designer: Michael Spencer
Lighting Designer: Nick Sharton

Martina Hildebrandt

Yerma / Federico Garcia Lorca

Michael and Michael
Southwark Playhouse - London
September 1995

Left: Act 3, scene 2: Masked dancers

Martina Hildebrandt: 'Although the auditorium seating was flexible, there was no way of avoiding the unusual architectural features of the venue: three prominent 30cm square pillars within the performance area, which at that time held the theatre's roof up! With a cast of nine, very little room backstage, a tiny budget and the need to keep any scene changes to a minimum, we chose to use these pillars as space definers rather than consider them a hindrance.'

Director: Michael Cabot
Designer: Martina Hildebrandt
Lighting Designer: Stuart Stocks

once upon a time

Once upon a time conjures up a magical world of imaginary plots and characters...but perhaps all performance is once upon a time. Myths, fairy stories, legends and topical satire are all rooted in an aural tradition and, like novels, they create pictures in the minds of readers and listeners. Theatre re-presents these tales using visual storytelling. The visual language is heightened and replaces verbal description of the location, atmosphere, character, status and time. Stylisation, visual symbols, metaphors and jokes are part of the design vocabulary in the work shown in this section.

It is also often technically demanding, requiring the juxtaposition of improbables and the translation of verbal images into visual ones. Transformations, quick-changes, swimming, flying, disappearing, fantastical and animal props and costumes all require design logic as well as solutions. These are action stories in which the designer can give clear information about character and location, allowing the narrative to proceed apace.

Ali Allen and Marise Rose

Lord of the Flies / William Golding, adapted by Nigel Williams

Pilot Theatre Company
Theatre Royal - York
September 1998

Ali Allen / Marise Rose: The challenges presented by *Lord of the Flies* provoked the evolution of a design in which physical theatre combines with structures inspired by images of wreckage to create a disturbing and savage environment. A revolving, pivoting tailplane and the ribs of a broken fuselage form an island, embedded in a sea of blue. By moving and turning these elements, the performers transform the space into island, hill, jungle, taking us on a journey through a landscape of beauty and terror.

Director: Marcus Romer
Set Designers: Ali Allen and Marise Rose
Costumer Designer: Jim O'Reilly
Lighting Designer: David Martin
Construction Designer: Bryan Tweddle
Photographer: Simon Warner

Elizabeth Ascroft

ALICE'S ADVENTURES IN WONDERLAND

DOWN THE RABBIT HOLE.

ACT ONE.

A CONSTANT IDENTITY SCRABBLE

COMPASS POINT MOBILE

CONTINUOUS TIME CONDUCTED BY WIND

TIME BY TEMPO

ROTATING AUTOMATED WEATHER VANE

TIME BY

ROTATING DETERMINED AN ORBITING SUN & MOON

Alice's Adventures in Wonderland
Lewis Carroll, adapted by Liz Ascroft, Lesley Chenery, Ian Forrest and James Mackie

The Duke's Playhouse
Open air promenade season, Williamson Park - Lancaster
July 1997

Elizabeth Ascroft: 'We decided that the audience should follow Alice down the rabbit hole - a daylight journey of 15 minutes and 100 metres amongst trees and Rhododendron. I wanted to make it feel like the time and space that falls between reality and dream; a 'non' space where anything is possible, because nothing is constant. All sense of time, space, direction and identity were tampered with, enabling everyone who made the journey with Alice to experience her feelings of disorientation and confusion.'

Director: Ian Forrest
Designer: Elizabeth Ashcroft
Lighting Designer: Brent Lees
Choreographer: Lorelei Lynn
Composer: James Mackie

David Collis

Toad, disguised

The Wind in the Willows
Kenneth Grahame, adapted by
Andy Rashleigh

Liverpool Playhouse
January 1996

Left: Toad disguised

David Collis: 'The whole production was set in a child's nursery, but three times normal size. This diminished the actors to toy-like proportions. All the various locations sprang from the objects within the room: the toy cupboard was Badger's house and the toy box became Mole's home and the jury box. The animals were dressed as humans with variations on the flat cap to denote and define their differing species.'

Director: Richard Williams
Designer: David Collis
Lighting Designer: David Horne
Choreographer: Terry John Bates
Photographer: Stephen James,
Prudence Cuming Associates

Sue Condie

Water - Seller

Princess Badr - Al - Badur

Aladdin / Jan Page

New Vic Theatre - Newcastle under Lyme
November 1997

Left: Water seller transformed into
Princess Badr-Al-badur

Sue Condie: 'This version of Aladdin is a magical story set once upon a time in an exotic land far, far away. Each of the characters is a trader in the Grand Bazaar. Their basic clothes reflect their trades, linking up with their stalls, which display their wares and which remain on stage throughout. As the story unfolds, the actors take on the roles of characters in Scheherazade's story, transforming mostly on stage by adding layers of costume and accessories. Aladdin was a musical feast of colour and richness taking the audience to another time, another place'

Director: Chris Martin
Set Designer: Lis Evans
Costume Designer: Sue Condie

Gabriella Csanyi-Wills

The Mikado / Gilbert and Sullivan

Opera della Luna
Touring
1998 - 1999

Left: Act 1 Three little maids

Gabriella Csanyi-Wills: 'As the action takes place in Koko, the tailor's, workshop/showroom, the design for the set was based on different fabrics - from the clouds to the flower beds. The ultimate criteria were flexibility, accessibility, fun and the fact that it all had to fit inside a Luton van. In Act 1, Koko's workshop, the space was cut into work zones by variously sized boxes containing "work material". Turning them over created a catwalk which opened up the space for greater fluidity of action. In Act 2, Koko's garden, hedges of green embossed velvet closed the space down again, creating a more intimate personal world and accentuating the impact of the Mikado's invasion of it.'

Director: Jeff Clarke
Designer: Gabriella Csanyi-Wills
Lighting Designer: Guy Dickens
Choreographer: Jenny Arnold
Photographer: Laurence Burns

Justine Gordon-Smith

In Xanadu / Pete Brooks

Hoxton Hall Community Theatre - London
November 1997

Left: The angel with the lost child in the petrified forest

Justine Gordon-Smith: 'Once upon a time, a girl called Esmerelda lived in a tower block in Haggerston. One day she fell asleep in the cinema and awoke to find herself in the Court of Kblai Khan. She was forced to tell stories of her travels, but unfortunately, she had never known anywhere but Hackney. Based on Italo Calvino's novel *Invisible Cities*, the text and the design explored Esmerelda's imagination and wit in her response to the everyday world around her. In this scene she travels to the forest where the living bury the dead, hoping that they will grow again and the tale swallows its own tail.'

Director: Pete Brooks
Designer: Justine Gordon-Smith
Lighting Designer: Ben Radcliffe
Music: Peter Cload
Photographer: Simon Camper

Gabriella Ingram

The Tales of Hoffmann / Jacques Offenbach

Opera Box
Swan Theatre - Stratford upon Avon and touring
May 1998

Left: Olympia, the doll and Spalanzani, the inventor

Gabriella Ingram: 'A magical moment when time and reality are suspended. Hoffmann has put on his magic spectacles and Olympia is finally presented. Within minutes the glasses are broken, the doll smashed and reality restored. Hoffmann realises he has fallen in love with a doll. I set this scene in the 18th century with the costumes, like the music, light, bright and fantastical. Olympia is a china doll in blue and white and Spalanzani's costume is printed with strange scientific instruments and a science book hat.'

Director: Brendan Wheatley
Designer: Gabriella Ingram
Lighting Designer: Ian Andrews
Photographer: Dave Smith

Christine Marfleet

If You Go Down To The Woods Tonight
Ellie Parker, with Christine Marfleet and Andrew Morris

Arts in Action and Music Pool
Queenswood Arboretum - Hereford
August 1998

Above: Finding Elizabeth

Christine Marfleet: 'If you go down to the woods ... elements from a night time walk in Queenswood - the journey of a lost child encountering strange, connected and disconnected spaces; observing past and present; glimpsing a potential future. Spanning several acres, this site offered an opportunity to devise images that would exist for the time taken to walk the child's journey, as striking, lasting memories of a place and performance.'

Director: Ellie Parker
Designer: Christine Marfleet
Production Assistants: Ian Buchanan, Hilary Groves, Udi Regev, Jessica Jones, Cathy Goodwin
Photographer: Jane Fleet

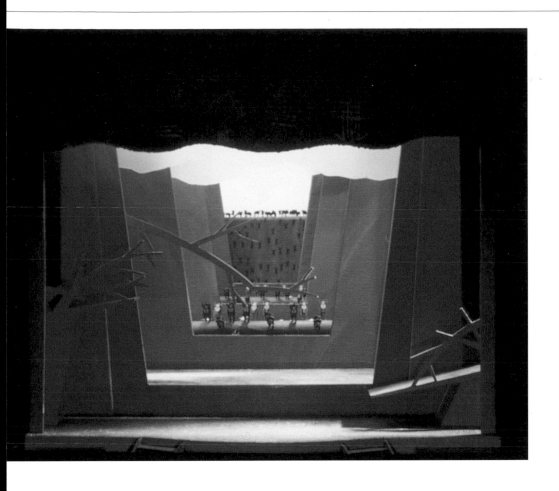

The Lion King
Roger Allers and
Irene Meechi, adapted by
Elton John and Tim Rice

Disney Theatrical
Productions
New Amsterdam Theatre,
Broadway - New York
November 1997

Far Left: The Dawn
Below far left: Rafiki's Tree
Left: Wildebeest Stampede
Below left: Elephant's
Graveyard

Richard Hudson:

'My challenge was to evoke
the vast African landscape
within the limitations of real
stage space. The "Eureka"
moment came from studying
African textiles. Their pure,
abstract patterns inspired
me to strip away everything
non-essential in the staging;
to use simple shapes and
bold colours that resonated
emotionally as well as
stylistically.'

Director:
Julie Taymor
Set Designer:
Richard Hudson
Costume Designer:
Julie Taymor
Mask and Puppet Designers:
Julie Taymor / Michael Curry
Lighting Designer:
Donald Holder
Choreographer:
Garth Fagan

Honk! / George Stiles and Anthony Drewe

Stephen Joseph Theatre - Scarborough
December 1997

Peter McKintosh: 'Honk! is a witty, musical
re-working of the ugly duckling story - a life
journey from outsized egg to beautiful swan and
a quest for acceptance. Set in and around the
duck pond and needing to flow smoothly from
one scene to the next, I decided to flood the
Stephen Joseph Theatre with cartoon water and
then float various oversized pieces of furniture on
it to create each new scene, whilst emphasising
animal versus human scale.'

Director: Julia McKenzie
Designer: Peter McKintosh
Lighting Designer: Kath Geraghty
Choreographer: Aletta Collins

*These images have been sponsored by
Imagination Entertainments*

Madeleine Millar

Tidelines / Mary Cooper and Gary Yershon

West Yorkshire Playhouse Theatre in Schools
Touring schools - Leeds
April 1996

Left: Maggie realises where Jaques will be - on his rock - and the tide is rising.

Madeleine Millar: 'Two people coming to terms with the pain of loss and separation: one old, one young. One uses her mother tongue, talks to her dead husband because: "On oublie très vite when you've no one to speak with." The other relives the conversations that lead to the break-up between his French dad and his English mum, "throwing stones at the sea like he's trying to hold back the tide." Together they repaint *The Secret*, the perfect marriage between English and French boat building, ready to sail her by the next high tide. From a wet afternoon to a warm mid-May morning, from neap tide to "the tide's rising. You can smell it. Summer again". Time and tide, healing.'

Director: Gail McIntyre
Set Designer: Madeleine Millar
Photographer: Simon Warner

Dody Nash

Hansel and Gretel / Engelbert Humperdink adapted by Steve Moffitt and Alex Ingram

The Baylis Programme, English National Opera
The ENO Works - London
November 1998

Dody Nash: 'A promenade production which transformed the audience into characters in a world, where time is fictive and magical. The woodcutter's cottage had a gritty, homemade texture. Illustrational costumes used second-hand materials to transform the everyday into the otherworldly. Hansel and Gretel wore real clothes, cut up, dyed and sewn back together with coloured threads. In the forest, Gretel ties flowers together to imagine a dancing man.'

Director: Steve Moffitt and Michael Walling
Set Designer: Fred Marchal
Costume Designer: Dody Nash
Lighting Designer: Matt Atwood
Photographer: Dee Conway

This image has been spsonosred by the Baylis Programme, ENO

Celia Perkins

Aladdin / Kenneth Alan-Taylor

Coliseum Theatre - Oldham
December 1997

Left and below left: In Widow Twanky's laundry

Celia Perkins: 'Designing for the Coliseum involves constant contrasts and extremes, working to tight deadlines on productions which are subject to the scrutiny and high expectations of a loyal audience - be they six years old or sixty. Panto is a production minefield. Designing starts in May; backcloths, costumes and scenery in July and the process continues until December, in tandem with the Coliseum's other main house shows. It is a miserable winter's night, but pantomime takes you into a world where anything could happen, reason flies out of the window and your optic nerves and lungs are forced into overtime.'

Director: Kenneth Alan-Taylor
Designer: Celia Perkins
Lighting Designer: Mark Howarth
Choreographer: Sheila Carter
Sound Designer: Jezz Hellins

Celia Perkins

Red Riding Hood / Stephen Christopher

Salamander Theatre Company
Chiswick Town Hall Theatre - London
December 1998

Jason Redgrave: 'Sketchbook note, 27 October 1998: a new idea - take inspiration from the lights in the auditorium for the forest. Hanging globes arranged like a chandelier could represent a canopy of trees on stage; by continuing these tree balls out into the auditorium so, by the time they have reached the last row of the auditorium lights, there are no tree balls, we could dispense with the usual notion of trees (and panto trees in particular) and tie the two spaces - auditorium and stage - together.'

Director: Stephen Christopher
Designer: Jason Redgrave
Lighting Designers: Esther Heaslip and Jason Larcombe

Isabel Robson

Hyratool Abror / Alisher Navoi

Tashkent State Russian Youth Theatre
Turkiston Theatre - Uzbekistan
November 1997

A UNESCO-Aschberg stage design
residency

Isabel Robson: 'The *laukhil* is a central
Asian, folding bookstand, symbolic for
supporting the Qu'ran. From page to
stage, the actors inhabited the magnified
structure in the telling of Navoi's Uzbeck
fables.'

Director: Nabi Abdurachmanov
Co-Director: Abror Yuldashev
Set Designer: Isabel Robson
Costume Designer: Kamilla Yakubova

Jason Redgrave

Alan Schofield

Georgina Shorter

The Lion, the Witch and the Wardrobe
CS Lewis, adapted by Irita Kutchmy

The Trinity Theatre - Tunbridge Wells
December 1997

Above: Act 1, scene 6 The wood in Narnia

Georgina Shorter: 'The objectives of this production were to capture containment, suspense, magic and curiosity. Containment was achieved with the use of four 5.5 metre high wardrobe doors, which provided the barrier between the present time - the 1940s - and the magical world of Narnia. In Narnia, the audience was greeted by a playground. This consisted of a series of hollow structures, with underground tunnels, which gave the performers the opportunity to explore the different routes they could travel. It was imperative that there should be elements which helped the cast and audience realise the progression of time, travel and change of season. These feelings were created by the constant and subtle lighting changes, the movement of the lamp post, and winter-shrouded trees which shed their cloths for spring.'

Directors: Francesca Gilpin / Caroline Elliott
Designer: Georgina Shorter
Lighting Designer: Bruce J Williams
Choreographer: Sally Coppen

This image has been sponsored by Terry Murphy Scenery Ltd

Mediaeval Banquet
A themed entertainment

Best Events Ltd of Maidenhead
The Great Room, Grosvenor House Hotel
London
January 1998

Alan Schofield: 'This was not a conventional theatre production, but a banquet with entertainment for 800 Japanese guests. Time and space presented two major problems. First, there was only a four hour get-in period to set up the entire event in the Great Room, which measured 50m x 24m. Secondly, the stage and dining tables occupied all the available floor space eliminating the possible use of three dimensional sets. The solution was to surround the diners with a continuous wrap-round painted canvas scene, 150m long by 5m high, hung from the gallery. '

Director: Deidre Dee
Set Designer: Alan Schofield
Costume Designer: Best Events Ltd
Scenic Artists: Alan Schofield / Natalie Penney

Justine Gordon-Smith

Tales of a Bald Headed Boy
Translated from the Turkish by Umut Ugur

Green Candle Dance Company,
Islington Arts Festival
June 1998

Justine Gordon-Smith: 'The place was based on a Turkish folk character, Kellogan, who lived on his wits and opened people's eyes to their own hearts. My designs were very much influenced by the novel, *On The Road to Baghdad*, which fused past and present characters, myths, colours, events and imagery to create a modern narrative. We wanted people literally to turn the corner within the performance and discover real and imaginary space. The costume design for the Giants is a true example of the fusion between the imagination of director, performer, designer and maker.'

Choreographer and Director: Fergus Early
Designer: Justine Gordon-Smith
Additional choreography: Phillipa Donella
Composer: Sally Davis
Photographer: Hugo Glendinning

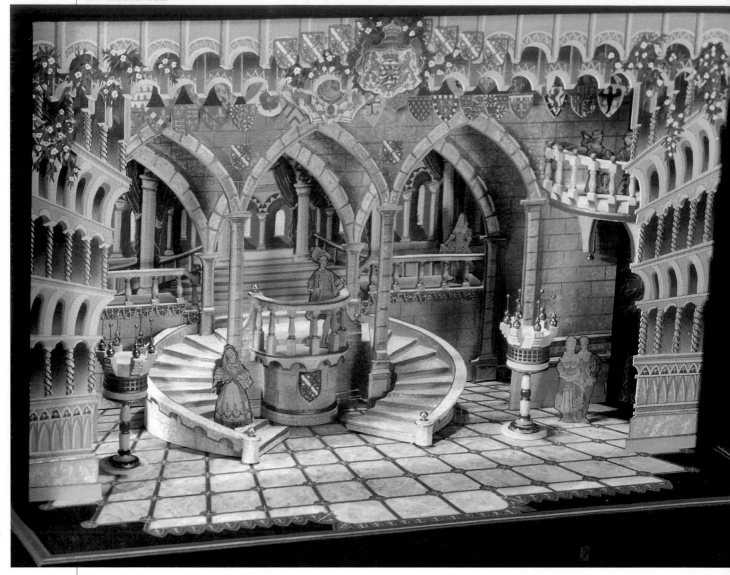

Babes in the Wood / David Lambert

Theatre Royal - Norwich
December 1998

Ian Westbrook: 'Pantomime is a uniquely
British tradition and gives many of us in the
theatre regular work. This is why I have chosen a
pantomime - it encompasses all the visual craft
and design skills. This finale model of *Babes in
the Wood* was inspired by Norwich Cathedral
and all the ecclesiastical decoration within it.
I also believe that pantomimes should have a
grand "walk down" for their finales, if only to show
off the frocks.'

Directors: Desmond Barrit and Peter Wilson
Set Designer: Ian Westbrook
Costume Designer: Diane Martin
Lighting Designers: Ian Greves and
Ian Westbrook
Choreographer: Bill Deamer
Producer: Roger Richardson

This image has been sponsored by 3D Creations

periods recreated

We can read character and status in each other's clothing and possessions, but how do we read apparently historically accurate costumes and settings from another period? We cannot see with the eyes of any era but our own and it is not possible to present a play or opera as it would have been presented when first written. It is equally impossible to present a period without contemporary overtones and interpretation. But it can be fascinating for a designer to research the period around a particular play, asking not only what the characters wore, but how and where they lived and how we might read this information from our own contemporary reference points. The work in this section is not characterised as historical reproduction, but is referring specifically to a particular period, with the designer making informed decisions about how to present the relevant material from it. The audience is invited to respond to the performance within a frame of reference which recreates a period play, opera, or ballet in our own or another period which will be illuminating.

Romeo and Juliet / William Shakespeare

The King's Head - London
June 1997

Above: Act 1, scene 1: Capulet

Anne Curry: 'The period is 1690s: adopting a frivolous decorative style to contrast with the tragedy of the story. This moment is the first entrance of Old Capulet in his gown, with a servant in the background. The costumes have to embody both character and status. The setting was a simple curtain so the costumes and wigs, make up and props needed to aid the narrative.'

Director: Dan Crawford
Set Designer: Nigel Hook
Costume Designer: Anne Curry

The Country Wife / William Wycherley

Stratford Festival - Ontario
June 1995

Above: Act 1, scene 1: Dorilant

Ann Curtis: 'Wycherley's 1670s social satire is peopled with timeless rogues, both men and women, cheating, whoring, drunken, self-seeking and outrageously witty and colourful behind a fragile mask of 'virtue'. Though in 17th-century dress, we can still recognise these types and we laugh, but the ending is as uncompromisingly cynical as the opening lines.'

Director: Douglas Campbell
Set Designer: John Leberg
Costume Designer: Ann Curtis
Lighting Designer: Harry Frehner
Photographer: Avon Studios,
Stratford-upon-Avon

Tim Goodchild

The Relapse or Virtue in Danger
John Vanbrugh

Royal Shakespeare Company
Swan Theatre - Stratford upon Avon
May 1995

Tim Goodchild: 'We added a few large props to the bare brick walls and timber balconies of the Swan, to recreate the faded grandeur of an 18th-century theatre. These included six huge chandeliers, which could be raised and lowered to denote time and space. As the audience entered, the candelabras, almost touching the floor, were raised high into the eves, to announce the beginning of the play.'

Director: Ian Judge
Designer: Tim Goodchild
Lighting Designer: Simon Tapping
Photographer: Donald Cooper

Judith Croft.

Laughter on the 23rd Floor / Neil Simon

Paddy Wilson and Laurence Myers in association with Yvonne Arnaud Theatre
Touring
August 1996

Judith Croft: 'This play is about *The Max Prince Show* - cult viewing in the 1950s - a crazy and unique crowd of writers, well paid, egocentric and above all funny, shut up in a room in New York on the 23rd floor. A space so important it features in the title, a period show set in its own time, to be enjoyed in ours. I imagined an Art Deco skyscraper dressed up with 50s style, with the buildings outside as a three-dimensional pattern echoing the floor. This moment catches Max Prince played by Gene Wilder, in despair at yet another appalling sketch.'

Director: Roger Haines
Designer: Judith Croft
Lighting Designer: Nick Richings

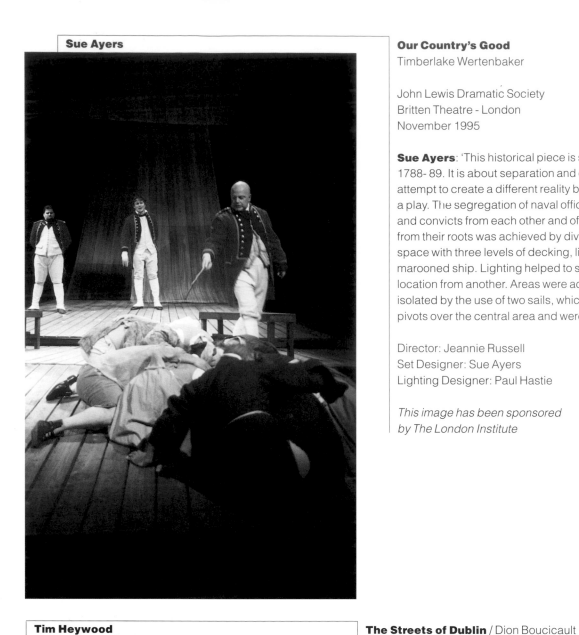

Sue Ayers

Our Country's Good
Timberlake Wertenbaker

John Lewis Dramatic Society
Britten Theatre - London
November 1995

Sue Ayers: 'This historical piece is set in 1788- 89. It is about separation and one man's attempt to create a different reality by presenting a play. The segregation of naval officers, soldiers and convicts from each other and of all of them from their roots was achieved by dividing the space with three levels of decking, like a marooned ship. Lighting helped to separate one location from another. Areas were additionally isolated by the use of two sails, which hung on pivots over the central area and were lowered in.'

Director: Jeannie Russell
Set Designer: Sue Ayers
Lighting Designer: Paul Hastie

This image has been sponsored by The London Institute

Tim Heywood

The Streets of Dublin / Dion Boucicault

Brixton Shaw
The Brix - London
December 1997

Tim Heywood: A magical romp through Victorian melodrama, seen with very modern eyes. The costumes reflected the beauty of the beauty of the Victorian silhouette, a Dickensian delight in truly tattered waifs and strays and an expression of overt theatricality with bustles and frocks galore. A magical past time.

Director: Judith Roberts
Set Designer: Charlotte Van Der Geest
Costume Designer: Tim Heywood
Lighting Designer: Nick Beadle

MR PUFFY · THE STREETS OF DUBLIN · TIM HEYWOOD 97

William Boldwood * Gabriel Oak * Bathsheba Everdene * Francis Troy * Fanny Robin

Far from the Madding Crowd
Thomas Hardy, adapted by Mark Ryan

Snap Theatre Company
Touring
February 1998

Nancy Surman: 'The adapter was interested in exploring the potential of some of the minor characters in Hardy's novel. So the story of Bathsheba and her three suitors is told under the night sky, over the course of an evening, by the farm workers of Weatherbury. This gave us the opportunity to explore the comedy in Hardy's original work and to comment on the behaviour and disposition of the principal protagonists. It also allowed us to play out Hardy's turbulent tale of human fallibility against the greater tableaux of nature and the eternal cosmic scale of the universe.'

Director: Andy Graham
Designer: Nancy Surman
Lighting Designer: Bob Bustance

These images have been sponsored by Snap Theatre Company

Tanya McCallin

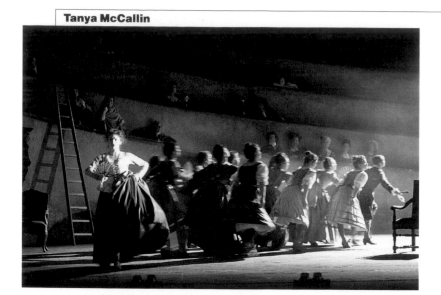

Manon / Jules Massenet

English National Opera
London Coliseum
May 1998

Left: Overture - dancers and chorus

Tanya McCallin: 'Over six Acts, Manon journeys from young country virgin to her death through the many levels of early 18th-century, French society. It is seedy, lustful and ultimately tragic; peopled by artisans, artists, performers, whores, gangsters, aristocrats and the bourgeoisie. David McVicar wanted this society on stage throughout, participating in Manon's story or voyeuristically observing it. The curved arena, with tiered seating, provided a universal space for the action - with spectators. Performers could move into the acting area through many stairways and entrances, allowing scene changes and action to be continuous. Furniture and props were reused in different configurations for different moments in the drama. Only Manon changed costume to show the development of time or place, the Chorus remaining in character throughout. Lighting was hugely important in defining time, space, focus and atmosphere.'

Director: David McVicar
Designer: Tanya McCallin
Lighting Designer: Paule Constable
Choreographer: Michael Keegan-Dolan
Photographer: William Rafferty

Dominie Hooper

The Daughter in Law / DH Lawrence

Octagon Theatre - Bolton
March 1998

Dominie Hooper: 'Set in a small mining village, circa 1911, the backdrop of heavily layered, textured fabric, sculpted mounds of coal and twisted metal structures retained the idea of industry set against nature. Together with devised lighting these served as an emotional landscape to the piece, rather than one that was purely visual. Requiring both a traditional and a more formal kitchen, this scene change between the two was solved by trucking the chimney to a different angle and swivelling the dresser to reveal the more upmarket bureau. Along with different props and furniture this effectively changed the space.'

Director: Joanna Read
Designer: Dominie Hooper
Lighting Designer: Fiona Lewry

Robin Linklater

Boston Early Music Festival and
Drottningholm Court Theatre
Sweden
June 1997

Left: Party time in Hades

Robin Linklater: 'This co-production aimed to recreate Rossi's huge, lavish 17th-century court spectacular for a modern audience. None of the original designs by Torelli have survived. The 1640s were a time of change for French theatre as Cardinal Mazarin was importing Italian artists with new ideas. This opera is a tragicomedia, with burlesque scenes woven into the story to highlight the tragedy.'

Director: Jack Edwards
Designer: Robin Linklater
Lighting Designer: L Stacy Eddy
Choreographer: Lucy Graham
Music Directors: Paul O'Dette and Stephen Stubbs

Becky Hawkins

Korczak / Nick Stimson and Chris Williams

The Young Company, Theatre Royal
The Drum Theatre - Plymouth and touring Poland
July 1997 (world premiere)

Becky Hawkins: '*Korczak* is a true story set in the Warsaw ghetto, celebrating the triumph of the human spirit. The script plays with time, memories, dreams and stories and this was reflected in the set - a flexible space with different levels that could accommodate the cast of 40 and allow the action to flow. We combined the emotional with the practical: a place of nightmares and universal fears; bleak towering walls, concealed doors, twisted skeletal metalwork; all changed dramatically by light, merging literal and mental environments.'

Director: Nick Stimson
Designer: Becky Hawkins
Lighting Designer: Tim Skelly
Photographer: Adam Eastland

Martin Johns

The Late Edwina Black / William Dinner and William Morum

Century Theatre, Rawnsley Centre - Keswick
July 1998

Martin Johns: 'The challenge was to accommodate three productions, on a converted stage, in a temporary space in a school. We had a one hour turnaround every other day. The locations included a 1990s patio and garage with car; an English bookshop and an American apartment, 1940 -1970; and a Victorian drawing room. The solution was to make all elements truckable and reversible.'

Director: Ian Forrest
Designer: Martin Johns
Lighting Designer: Ian Townsend
Photographer: Ian Tilton

Liam Doona

Frankenstein / Mary Shelly, adapted by Richard Hurford

Theatre Royal - York
November 1997

Liam Doona: 'In a frozen moment before his own death at the hands of "The Creature", Frankenstein encounters the ghosts of his murdered family. Retribution, responsibility and scientific advancement are brought to sudden, silent collision inside a monumental steel chamber, ruptured by advancing ice at the heart of the Antarctic. The original score provides an acute sense of loss, whilst the lighting emphasises the scale of the catastrophe. The Creature observes and waits his moment ...'

Director: Damian Cruden
Designer: Liam Doona
Lighting Designer: Peter Higton
Composer: Christopher Maidin

time transposed

Transformation is an essential element of performance. It relishes the juxtaposition of the before and after and the requirement for it presents designers with a series of questions that will influence their creative decisions. This section includes work in which a design or production decision transposes a piece from the time in which it was written or set, into another time frame or composite of time information. The rearrangement of time within a piece and as a production device is a storyteller's decision. The story told in performance has a 'slant' on it, either through a character or narrator, or through an applied context. The design can become a form of interpretation. What is meant by that image, in that context? How might moving it to another time or place make it more meaningful for this audience, here and now? What are our connections with or analogies to that situation, to those characters?

Theatre design is about the making of meaning, by looking through the eyes of another time and context, and by considering the nature of the changes made to characters and surroundings through time and their experience.

Luca Antonucci

Le Due Contesse / I Due Baroni
Giovanni Paisiello / Domenico Cimarosa

La Societa dell'opera Buffa
Theatre of Casalmaggiore
November 1996

Left, from top to bottom: The Garden
and The Villa in *Le Due Contesse*, The
Garden and The Great Salon in *I Due
Baroni*

Luca Antonucci: 'These two 18th-
century operas were conceived as a
single project, using the same basic set
and they were performed in one evening.
In *Le Due Contesse*, the space is defined
by a graphic treatment on the wall panels.
The cut-out, paper-like, black and white
costumes appear as if from an 18th-
century *bonbonnière*. In *I Due Baroni*, the
space is deconstructed and the structure
is finally revealed. Whilst the space keeps
its original proportions it changes radically
in its spatiality. The set becomes a circus-
like platform and the 19th-century
costumes push the setting forward in
time.'

Director: Gino Zampieri
Designer: Luca Antonucci
Conductor: Allessandro Sangiorgi
Lighting Designer: Daniele Naldi

Elroy Ashmore

Rockin' Mikado / Michael Poyner and Mark Dougherty after Gilbert and Sullivan

Ulster Theatre Company
Waterfront Hall - Belfast and touring
August 1998

Elroy Ashmore: 'Gilbert and Sullivan's *Mikado* looked at Japan through Victorian eyes and values. *Rockin' Mikado* takes place in contemporary Japan, only to find the country looking back 20-30 years: Elvis lives; Punk tribal groups perform all Sunday at Yoyogi-Koen Park; motorbikes, leather jackets and greased hair are all in high fashion. The production was set in a complex textural world of information: banners flutter in the Waterfront auditorium and on stage; mobile phones ring and fax machines chatter. The set overpowers the only traditional icon - a Japanese pavilion - on which the band plays. All this with the Northern Irish accents and many references to the complex world of Irish politics.'

Director: Michael Poyner
Designer: Elroy Ashmore
Lighting Designers: Keith Shanks and Michael Poyner
Choreographer: Anne-Marie Brady

Atlanta Duffy

Iphigenia / Che Walker, after Euripides

Bat Productions
Southwark Playhouse - London
May 1998

Left: Old Man and Orestes

Atlanta Duffy: 'Thousands of unseen soldiers wait at the water's edge for the wind that will take their ship to war. Time is suspended. We transformed the small, low-ceilinged space into the army encampment of the play's setting. We took out all the seats and sat the audience on concrete breakers. Three and a half tonnes of sea pebbles and filthy scraps of carpet littered with fag ends helped evoke the stagnant, restless world into which Iphigenia and her mother Clytemnestra have been summoned.'

Director: Benjamin May
Designer: Atlanta Duffy
Lighting Designer: Tim Bray
Music: James Gray and Richard Pitt
Photographer: Robert Workman

Three Hours After Marriage

Gay, Pope and Arbuthnot

Royal Shakespeare Company
Swan Theatre - Stratford-upon-Avon
May 1996

Tim Goodchild: 'Yet another Restoration romp! Having just designed *The Relapse* for the Swan, I wanted to change the period and the time frame and create another world entirely. We decided to set it in a surreal, madcap world, around 1860. A claustrophobic, prison-like space was created from display cases, which were piled high and holding the grotesque antiquities and mutations for the central character, Dr Fossil. Floor traps, secret doors and hiding places were added to this and a huge clock, which dominated the set, ticked the passing of time throughout the play.

Director: Richard Cottrell
Designer: Tim Goodchild
Lighting Designer: Hugh Vanstone
Music: Mark Warman

Patrick Connellan

Richard Foxton

Julius Caesar
William Shakespeare

Birmingham Repertory Theatre
November 1997

Left: Act 5, scene 1: The plains of Philippi - Anthony, Cassius, Brutus and Octavius

Patrick Connellan: 'We created a banked arena that looked like a stadium/lecture theatre/ library or democratic assembly, based on the anatomical theatre at Guy's Hospital, London. The moment shown is of the parley before civil war ensues. The stadium has been divided into four, symbolising the hacked body of Caesar and the divisions between the armies. The time is multi-historical. The basis is England in the 1930s when sections of the ruling class were looking for a new Caesar. Rome was conjured up by senators donning togas over suits, like public school boys acting out the assassination in the school play. The soothsayer was the only character in modern dress.'

Director: Anthony Clark
Designer: Patrick Connellan
Lighting Designer:
Davy Cunningham
Photographer: Ivan Kyncl

Dancing at Lughnasa / Brian Friel

Octagon Theatre - Bolton
September 1996

Above: The narrator, Michael, remembers his childhood

Richard Foxton: 'I was interested in the subjective quality of memory - focusing on a collage of sharp images melding into each other, sometimes naturalistic, sometimes more lyrical. The kitchen fades into the garden, the moon and sky dissolve through a gauze, the cornfield and stone wall could onclose or be distant landscape tinged with the warmth of memory.'

Director: Ian Forrest
Designer: Richard Foxton
Lighting Designer: Fiona Lewry
Choreographer: Lorelei Lynn

A Mad World My Master
Thomas Middleton

Shakespeare's Globe Theatre - London
August 1998

Right: View from the Musicians' Gallery at the rear of the stage
Below right: Will Johnson as Follywit

Shakespeare's Globe is a round performance space, built of
oak and lime plaster, with a thatched roof over seating
galleries, but open to the elements above the 'groundlings',
who stand and move around the covered thrust stage in the
central yard.

Kandis Cook: 'Rather than fight the stage space, with its
pillars, palatial ceiling and background of doors, discovery
space and upper balcony, it seemed we should embrace this
opulence of colour and symbolic imagery, energy and the
pure meaning of the place. This we did by taking the colours
and knitting the threads into the action of this cynical and
darkly humorous story. It is a story of a furiously changing
society, giving opportunity to whoever could think fast
enough to clamber out of their present status - or lack of it -
and elevate themselves to the next rung, if not higher.'

Director: Sue Lefton
Designer: Kandis Cook
Music: Claire Van Kampen
Photographers: Chris Moyse and Richard Kalina

The Tempest / William Shakespeare

The New Vic Theatre - Newcastle under Lyme
March 1998

Lis Evans: 'The design was inspired by the way Prospero conjures with and manipulates the forces of nature. Reminiscent of the work of the artists Andy Goldsworthy and Richard Long, the setting was one of natural shapes and colours. Willow and hazel were woven into arches, wattles and sculptural pieces and painted wood and fabric were textured and layered to represent the vivid natural patterns found in rock forms and waves. For the costumes, the two distinctive cultures of the ship-wrecked party and the inhabitants of the island were distinguished on the one hand by the flamboyant style of the Napoleonic era and by the character, colours and textures and the 'strange nature' of the island on the other.'

Director: Peter Cheeseman
Designer: Lis Evans
Lighting Designer: Jo Dawson
Music: John Kirkpatrick
Sound: James Earls-Davis

Iph / Colin Teevan, after Euripides

Lyric Theatre - Belfast
March 1999

Gary McCann: 'Euripides' fable - a bleak vision of a society in which a man is prepared to sacrifice his own daughter to further the political ambitions of his nation - is updated to reflect the concerns of 21st-century Northern Ireland. The ultra-modern setting, which is vaguely reminiscent of Bilbao's Guggenheim Gallery, and the royal characters, dressed in the excesses of European haute couture, are in stark contrast to the chorus - a group of working class Belfast girls dolled up for a night on the razz.'

Director: David Grant
Designer: Gary McCann
Lighting Designer: Paul O'Neill

Passion / Stephen Sondheim and James Lapine

Bill Kenwright Ltd
Queen's Theatre - London
March 1996

Left: Model storyboard

Paul Farnsworth: 'Passion was set in Milan and a remote Italian military outpost in the 1860s and moved both forwards and backwards in time (to the 1840s) requiring numerous fluid changes between locations. Guided by the music, we had to be able to pass seamlessly from interiors to exteriors and back again, sometimes using an almost cinematic split-screen approach, in which two locations appeared together in the same space - the action of the plot being propelled by the reading and writing of letters by the main characters.'

Director: Jeremy Sams
Designer: Paul Farnsworth
Lighting Designer: Mark Henderson
Choreographer: Jonathan Butterell

Penny Fitt

Eastward Hoe! / George Chapman, Ben Johnson and John Marston

Bristol Old Vic
New Vic Studio - Bristol
November 1998

Penny Fitt: 'The text is self-consciously a theatrical presentation and the comedy in it very much a comment on the London of the day, 400 years ago. What I was attempting to create was less a set than a stage; a stage which could fuse our 20th-century studio space with the Blackfriars' stage of 1605 on which the play was originally performed. The map, inked across the wooden wall of our created theatre, laid out the geography for our 20th-century audience. All the street names in the script are in the A to Z. Four hundred years? No time at all!'

Director: John Hartoch
Designer: Penny Fitt
Lighting Designer: Vic Kilpatrick

Jane Frere

Jock

Raucle Carlin

Tam

The Merry Andrew

JGF

The Jolly Beggars / Robert Burns

Wildcat Theatre Company
The Cottier Theatre - Glasgow
October 1996

Jane Frere: 'A flashback from a contemporary opening takes us back to the Burns era, demanding the active transformation of the set, by the actors, to recreate the atmosphere of the 18th-century Poosie Nansie Inn. This touring production needed a simple, transportable set, so I created a wooden box, defining the tiny floorspace of the real inn in Ayrshire. It was like a puzzle to be reassembled and transformed - a magical box of tricks to allow the actors to tell their tale. To get a sense of the Jolly Beggars, I drew some inspiration from the characters living rough in doorways around Victoria Station. With their multiple layers of clothes, old and new, some in richly vibrant colours, others faded and threadbare, beggars have no choice but to wear all they own at the same time.'

Director: John Bett
Designer: Jane Frere
Lighting Designer: Craig Harrower
Musical Director: Ron Shaw
Photographer: Sean Hudson

Sotoba-Komachi - Hanjo / Yukio Mishima

Mamoru Iriguchi

Acting Company Mito
ACM Theater - Mito, Japan
March 1995

Mamoru Iriguchi: 'Both plays are about a woman who has been waiting for her lover for decades (or even longer). They were interpreted by the director as the stories told by three women imprisoned in a small room for a long time. To create a very intimate relationship between stage and audience, a tent with space for 50 people was built in the main house of the theatre. Everything in the tent was painted in tones of brown to make the whole scene resemble a very old photograph. '

Director: Naoko Kuboniwa
Design and Lighting: Mamoru Iriguchi

Robert Innes Hopkins

The Bartered Bride / Bedrich Smetana

Opera North
Grand Theatre - Leeds and touring
September 1998

Robert Innes Hopkins: 'We moved the action of the opera from the usual 19th-century setting to 1972. The permanent set was a makeshift stage erected on a piece of scrubland on the edge of town. The costumes were hideous Iron Curtain chic.'

Director: Daniel Slater
Designer: Robert Innes Hopkins
Lighting Designer: Simon Mills
Choreographer: Vanessa Grey

These images have been sponsored by Opera North

Venus and Adonis with **Dido and Aeneas** / John Blow and Henry Purcell

De Vlaamse Opera
The Opera House - Gent, Belgium
November 1996

Left: Cupid, Adonis and Venus
Below lefft: Scene 1, Dido and Aneas

Mark Jonathan: 'These two short operas were played without interruption in a single basic setting, based on the Greenwich Observatory. For Venus and Adonis, a 17th-century science fiction story, I needed a supernatural feel. I used HMI light to create mostly black and white images. Dido and Aeneas needed a completely different treatment. As the dramatic complexity developed I introduced more colour, in parallel with the opera's movement through time, from morning to sunset and encroaching night, and through space from Dido's Palace to the witches' lair, the hunt and storm, the apparition and the harbour. '

Director: Stephen Lawless
Set Designer: Benoît Dugardyn
Costume Designer: Lez Brotherston
Lighting Designer: Mark Jonathan
Choreographer: Andrew George
Conductor: René Jacobs
Photographer: Annemie Augustijns

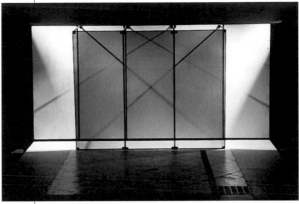

Fred Meller

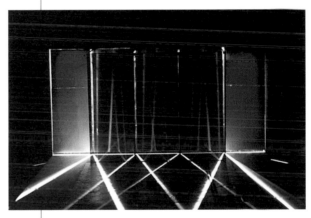

Othello / William Shakespeare

Theatre Royal - Bury St Edmunds and touring
August 1998

Fred Meller: 'A large Perspex panel, covered in black window film in front of panels of very thin birch wood, acted as a two-way mirror revealing a space in a different time. Venice was created by using a shiny black, reflective floor piece which evoked a dark, wet place. The birch wood was back lit in varying intensities to simulate the arid heat of Cyprus. The temptation scene was played in a steam room. Costumes and set paid homage to the early 1800s while we created a very contemporary feel through a positive design decision to use modern elements.'

Director: Colin Blumereau
Designer: Fred Meller
Lighting Designer: Mark Passey

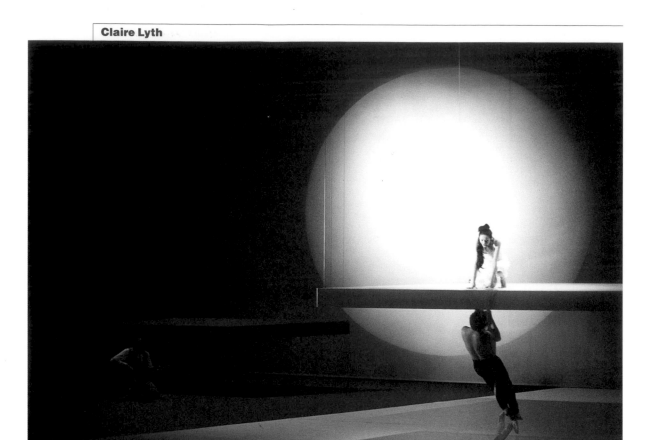

Romeo and Juliet / William Shakespeare

Sherman Theatre - Cardiff and touring
February 1995

Claire Lyth: 'Civil war: Shakespeare's play is
updated to 20th-century Spain. Spanish passion,
temperament and formality are portrayed
against a minimalist set of two cantilevered
platforms. The lovers are seen as small elements
in an almost empty space dominated by a cold
sun/moon. The area is divided diagonally into
white for the Capulets and black for the
Montagues. The colours are echoed in the
costumes, making any invasion of each other's
space more emphatic. The scene only alters for
the feast, when blood-red silks drop in and the
actors fill the space, dressed in flamboyant red,
fiesta-inspired costumes.'

Director: Glen Walford
Designer: Claire Lyth
Lighting Designer: Kevin Sleep

Top Girls / Caryl Churchill

Octagon Theatre - Bolton
March 1997

Jocelyn Meall: 'The play is set at the beginning
of the Thatcher years. It starts with a group of
historic women coming together to celebrate
Marlene's promotion up the capitalist ladder. The
Octagon Theatre was in thrust staging. The
space was altered for the different locations -
restaurant, office, back yard, kitchen - using just
furniture and doors. This was set against a
sculptural relief of a sleeping woman cradling a
child. The floor was a photographic collage of
important women from history. The relief was
carved from polystyrene, using chainsaws and
skimmed with muslin.'

Director: Lawrence Till
Designer: Jocelyn Meall
Lighting Designer: Fiona Lewry
Photographer: Ian Tilton

Ian Teague

Still Waters / Devised

Gwent Theatre Company
Touring
May 1995

Ian Teague: 'We stand in the midst of a technological revolution. This theatre in education programme examined the nature of technological change. The play focused on the building of the South Wales canal system and the effect of what was then 'new technology' on a cross section of society: the entrepreneurs and engineers, the navvies and those who lived and worked along the canal route. The set looked forward in time to the completed canal system and the impending industrial revolution. Taking a visual cue from de Loutherbourg's *Coalbrookdale by Night* the set provided a non-naturalistic space for this multi-location examination of a moment in time.'

Director: Gary Meredith
Set Designer: Ian Teague

Jocelyn Meall

Argan.   Beline.

Pwy Sy'n Sa / Molière double bill
in Welsh translation

Theatr Gwynedd - Bangor and touring
December 1994

Left: Y Claf Diglefydd
Middle left: Costumes for Y Claf Diglefydd
Bottom left: Costumes fo Doctor Di-glem

Martin Morley: 'This was a double bill of
Welsh language versions of *Le Malade
Imaginaire* (*Y Claf Diglefydd*) and *Le
Médecin Malgré Lui* (*Doctor Di-glem*). The
directors had very different approaches to
style and the meaning of period in the
context of a theatrical production. The
unifying visual factor was the basic
structure of the set, though each used it in
a different way. The costumes for *Y Claf
Diglefydd* were broadly traditional, i.e.
they treated time in an historical way. For
Doctor Di-glem, we raided period forms
and silhouettes and wedded them loosely
to modern fashion. The palette for *Y Claf
Diglefydd* was rich and the fabrics heavy.
In *Doctor Di-glem* it was sunny creams
and whites, with occasional flashes of
colour, and very lightweight fabrics. 'The
set was a 3D drawing, in steel, of a
classical room-cum-courtyard, behind
which was a double row of shuttered
windows. The stage floor was a formal
marbled pattern on MDF.'

Directors: Graham Laker and
Firenza Guidi
Designer: Martin Morley
Lighting Designer: Tony Bailey Hughes

*These images have been sponsored
by Cwmni Theatr Cymru and Theatr
Gwynedd*

Romeo and Juliet / William Shakespeare

Belgrade Theatre - Coventry
October 1997

Left: The Capulets' feast
Below left: Costumes for Lady Capulet,

Cathy Ryan: 'We wanted to set Romeo and Juliet in a world where society is struggling to maintain order in the aftermath of an abandoned, corrupt colonial rule, in a period (late 1950s) that would have recognisable similarities with the present. We hit on the idea of a fusion of Cuba, New Orleans, Mexico and Haiti - a place where the natural religion had been suppressed and over-layered with Catholicism. Hence, Friar Lawrence becomes a Santerian Priest, part Franciscan and part voodoo shaman. The Capulets' feast became a vibrant day of the dead carnival with painted skeletal masks and calypso dancing. The fights break out in the pool hall and the burials take place above ground preceeded by a slow jazz funeral procession.'

Director: Chris Monks
Designer: Cathy Ryan
Lighting Designer: Vince Herbert
Choreographer: Pat Garret
Fight Director: Rene Krupinski

Crivelli's Garden / Fiona Graham

Theatre Centre
Salisbury Playhouse, The Mercury Theatre - Colchester and touring
October 1996

Nettie Scriven: 'A fusion of forms, narrative and imagery, slip between the past, present and future. Images of Renaissance Italy, Salazar's Portugal, urban London. A live performance with video interventions, fluid and elusive, playing within a world of geometric and monolithic shapes. A year-long collaboration inspired by Paula Rego's triptych Crivelli's Garden (National Gallery). The creative process also involved development work in schools and colleges.'

Director: Rosanne Hutt
Designer: Nettie Scriven
Composer: Matthew Bailey
Video Artist: Jane Fitzgerald
Photographer: Hugh Glendinning

This image has been sponsored by Nottingham Trent University

Richard III / William Shakespeare

Haymarket Theatre - Leicester
October 1998

Above: Act 1, scene 3

Juliet Shillingford: 'We gave the play a
modern setting to make the set and
costumes as unobtrusive as possible to
the actors and audience. The metallic set
was based on some photographs I took of
buildings in the City of London, luminous
from a distance, or at night, but streaked
with stains and dirt close up. The set
created a semi-transparent barrier
through which some events could be
glimpsed beyond. In the final moments the
entire wall winched down slowly to create
a ramp with the balconies and pipes
becoming a landscape for the battle
scenes.'

Director: Paul Kerryson
Designer: Juliet Shillingford
Lighting Designer: Jenny Cane
Photograher: Stephen Vaughan

Louise Ann Wilson

Christopher Richardson

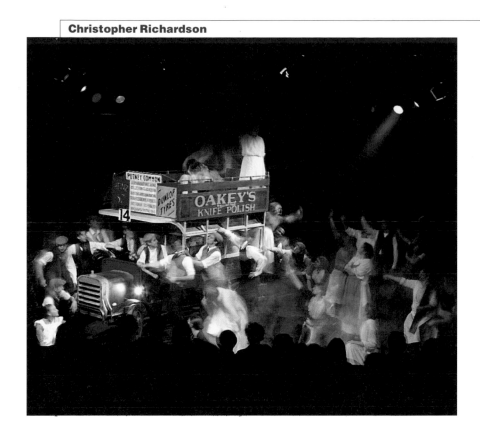

Pleasance Theatre
London
1995

Left: *Bus!* A Young Pleasance
production, January 1996

Christopher Richardson: The
timbered factory roof under which
the B type omnibus was born now
lends atmosphere to the Pleasance,
London. Fly rhomboids, not large
squares. 'Just like the Sydney
Opera House,' said Ralph Koltai.
The very quirkiness of the place
seems to bring out the best in
designers. Most may demand an
end-on stage, but the 10m x 10m
performance area can be adapted
to the round or to many a hybrid in
between. It cost £400,000 to
convert and equip and 280 seats
sold can cover the bills. Maybe it is
a space for the time and time for
such a space.

Designer: Christopher Richardson
and Dan Watkins for Theatre
Futures, with MEB Partnership
Architects
Engineers: DMP
Acoustics: APT

*This image has been sponsored by
Pleasance Theatre Festival*

House / Simon Armitage

WilsonWilson Company
Goldthorpes Yard - Huddersfield
October 1998

Left: In the bathroom, a man evolves from
ape to human

Louise Ann Wilson: '*HOUSE* was a site-
specific theatre event created for a 19th-century
worker's cottage. An audience of fifteen entered
a world where past, present and future existed
together. The production took a year to realise. It
embraced the house's 180-year history, yet took
us to the beginning of time. In the first room a
man, surrounded by his life, slept. Darwin and
Genesis provided literary clues to the distance
we would travel. In the bowels of the building a
preacher conjured up the swamp from which we
came. Fish swam in an ocean at our feet and rain
fell from the ceiling. Finally, in the most

dilapidated room, Adam and Eve sat, after
journeying home safe and sound following their
expulsion from Eden.'

Creator-Director: Wils Wilson
Creator-Designer: Louise Ann Wilson
Lighting Designer: Nigel Edwards
Composer: Robin Rimbaud aka Scanner
Photographer: Fiver

*This image has been sponsored by the
Lawrence Batley Theatre*

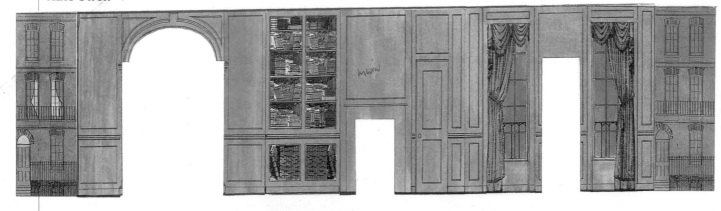

Move over Moriarty / Maggie Fox and
Sue Ryding

Lip Service
Rose Theatre - Ormskirk and touring
October 1996

Above: Artwork of double-sided flats for
the scene painter

Kate Owen: 'A comedy version of
Sherlock Holmes with two women playing
all the parts. First a prologue in Baker
Street, next a very small box set of Holmes'
study, complete with hidden passages,
which closes and spins around to reveal a
theatre, the middle of Dartmoor, a rail
carriage, a back-street and a hospital. The
female quick-change costumes have
vacuum-formed Edwardian bodices. This
show continues to play in small, medium
and large spaces, and fits-up in under two
hours.'

Director: Gwenda Hughes
Designer: Kate Owen
Lighting Designer: Nick MacLiammoir
Music: Mark Vibrans

Karen Frances Webber

The Caucasian Chalk Circle
Bertolt Brecht

Guildford School of Acting
The Electric Theatre - Guildford
September 1998

Left: The Fat Prince

Karen Frances Webber: 'Early on, the
director expressed a desire to maintain the
ancient Chinese element of the story. This
was achieved by using traditional masks
and formalised acting techniques for the
members of the court. As this approach
moved away from the tradition of Brechtian
theatre, it allowed us greater freedom with
the costumes, which became colourful and
eclectic, ranging from *Monty Python* to
Kabuki.

Director: Gordon McDougall
Set Designer: Alison Cartledge
Costume Designer: Karen Frances Webber
Lighting Designer: Neil Fraser

*This image has been sponsored by
Guildford School of Acting*

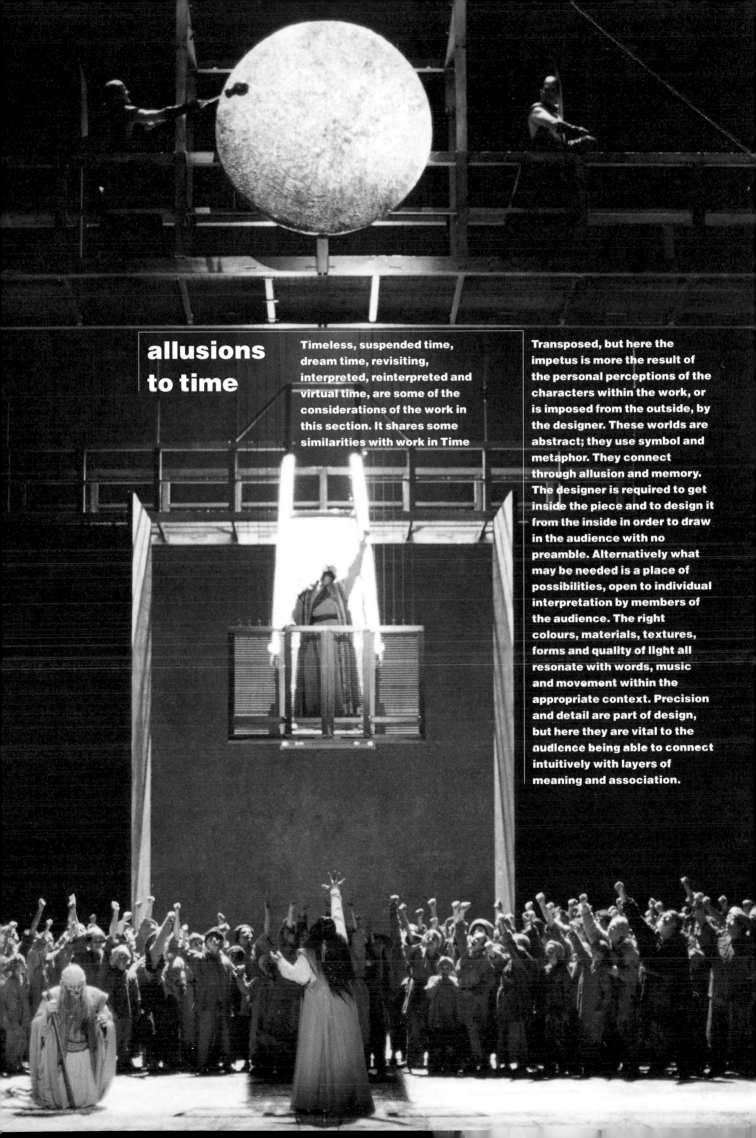

allusions to time

Timeless, suspended time, dream time, revisiting, interpreted, reinterpreted and virtual time, are some of the considerations of the work in this section. It shares some similarities with work in Time Transposed, but here the impetus is more the result of the personal perceptions of the characters within the work, or is imposed from the outside, by the designer. These worlds are abstract; they use symbol and metaphor. They connect through allusion and memory. The designer is required to get inside the piece and to design it from the inside in order to draw in the audience with no preamble. Alternatively what may be needed is a place of possibilities, open to individual interpretation by members of the audience. The right colours, materials, textures, forms and quality of light all resonate with words, music and movement within the appropriate context. Precision and detail are part of design, but here they are vital to the audience being able to connect intuitively with layers of meaning and association.

Jan Bee Brown

Othello / William Shakespeare

TAG Theatre Company
Citizen's Theatre - Glasgow and touring
September 1998

Left: Act 2, scene 1: Cyprus
Below left: Act 5, scene 2: Bedchamber

Jan Bee Brown: 'This was accessible Shakespeare for all ages, for a company with a large schools' audience and touring to medium-scale venues throughout Scotland. As the play is timeless, the design should portray no particular time and a single setting can be transformed with light to represent walls, streets, entrances, corridors, a pier, balcony and platform bed. The imagery of water flows through the text leading me to use gabion boxes - steel cages used in the real world as sea defences. Light, collapsible and tour-friendly they serve as a visual metaphor for the strength and fragility of love, whilst imprisoning characters in their shadows.'

Director: James Brining
Designer: Jan Bee Brown
Lighting Designer: Jeanine Davies
Original Music: Scientific Support Dept.
Photographer: Renzo Mazzolini

These images have been sponsored by TAG Theatre Company

Dawn Allsopp

I Have Been Here Before / JB Priestley

Swan Theatre - Worcester
October 1995

Dawn Allsopp: 'The play is set in the sitting room of The Black Bull Inn, North Yorkshire. It is 1937. Priestley is exploring the concept of cycles of time - that we may tread the same spiral track through life many times, before taking control and changing our destiny. I designed a room where naturalistic furniture stood on a floor of concentric clock faces, all slightly out of step with each other. A large window dominated the space with an abstracted moorland beyond. Inside walls were suggested by panels of peeling wallpaper.'

Director: Mark Babych
Designer: Dawn Allsopp
Lighting Designer: Christine Piper

Mark Bailey

Hadrian the Seventh / Peter Luke

Chichester Festival Theatre
April 1995

Left: Act 1, scene 3 The coronation of Hadrian

Mark Bailey: 'Hadrian the Seventh is a dream play, moving through time and space in the lead character's mind, from his squalid lodging room to the wealth and power of the Vatican. This transformation, achieved by the splitting of the back wall in the form of a crucifix, moves the action from a black void to a golden world peopled by the red figures of the Cardinals.'

Director: Terry Hands
Designer: Mark Bailey
Lighting Designer: Terry Hands

Robert Jones

Henry VIII or All is True / William Shakespeare

Royal Shakespeare Company
The Swan Theatre - Stratford-upon-Avon
November 1996

Left and above: Paul Jesson as Henry VIII

Robert Jones: 'This design was a response to the architecture of the Swan Theatre - the only obvious piece of "designed" scenery being two lead doors engraved with the original title of the play, All is True. The doors occasionally swung open to reveal a world of ostentatious pageantry; glimpses of royal propaganda staged in a sham and overtly theatrical style in stark contrast to the downstage realpolitik world of the court.'

Director: Gregory Doran
Designer: Robert Jones
Lighting Designer: Howard Harrison
Choreographer: Terry John Bates
Photographer: Ivan Kyncl

This exhibit has been sponsored by Royal Shakespeare Company

allusions to time

Le False Confidenze / Marivaux

Teatro Stabile di Genova
Teatro Duse - Genoa, Italy
October 1998

Hayden Griffin: 'The director and I decided to set this piece in a "corridor". The play develops in a series of chance meetings in a sort of limbo space; it was written long before Ibsen and therefore the need for realistic rooms or time elapses is unimportant. The corridor solution seemed to serve the final production well. Although the costumes reflect the period accurately, the space is more nebulous and, I hope, timeless.'

Director: Marco Sciaccaluga
Set Designer: Hayden Griffin
Costume Designer: John Bright
Lighting Designer: Sandro Sussi

Robert Cheesmond

The Rose Tattoo / Tennessee Williams

Theatr Clwyd - Mold
September 1995

Pamela Howard: 'Underneath a grim concrete motorway in America lies a small Sicilian enclave where the past and future is reality and the present does not exist. Serafina's house may be small and simple, but it expands with her memories, above all those of her deceased husband and her daughter Rosa, the living embodiment of the Rose Tattoo. Life is like a merry-go-round, a fairground of emotions and on this carousel the heart of a woman, Serafina, is shown. A wall of memories becomes an altar of dreams. The village community, dark and superstitious, is finally transported into the joy of the future.'

Director: Helena Kaut-Howson
Designer: Pamela Howard
Lighting Designer: Nic Beadle
Choreographer: Clive Mendus
Photographer: Nic Beadle

Reckless Saints / Amelia Morrey

Department of Drama, University of Hull
Donald Roy Theatre - Hull
November 1997

Left: McGantic's Invocation

Robert Cheesmond: 'A complex web of relationships is enacted between six people, two of whom emanate from the past, and four from the present. " I am Christy Corsay, skipped loose from Bedlam - a hundred years ago. I am not a ghost or a spirit, a figment of imagination, nor any hallucination - I just am - why not? I am concurrent ... " Two fictional spaces, a ruined asylum and a modern apartment, merge in the actuality of the theatre space, (re)constructed so as to place each audience member, unprotected by the security of conventional naturalistic form, squarely in the centre of dramatic action.'

Director: Robert Chessmond
Set Designer: Robert Chessmond
Costume Designer: Joanne Smith
Lighting Designer: David Horwell
Photographer: Ray Johnson,
of Hull Photographic Service

King Arthur / Henry Purcell and
John Dryden

Théâtre du Châtelet - Paris and
The Royal Opera House - London
February 1995

Left: Osmond, Knight, Guillamar
Below left: Matilda, Emmerline, Merlin

Paul Brown: '*King Arthur* is set in a
timeless, mythical world, where the action
needs to move rapidly from battlefields to
enchanted forests, from cornfields to
frozen wasteland and where finally Britain
needs to rise out of the sea. This was
achieved by reinventing the devices of the
theatre of Purcell's day, in a contemporary
style, in order to maintain the rhythm of the
piece. The opera's fabulous nature was
evoked by the costumes, layering sources
as diverse as Japan and Wales, on a stage
where a winged blitzed housewife shared
the space with medieval knights on
horseback.'

Director: Graham Vick
Designer: Paul Brown
Lighting Designer: Wolfgang Göbbel
Choreographer: Ron Howell
Design Assistant: Ros Coombs

Charles Cusick Smith

Marabou Stork Nightmare / Irvine Welsh,
adapted by Harry Gibson

Leicester Haymarket with G & J Productions
August 1996

Charles Cusick Smith: 'Time: the present - a
young man, Roy Strang, is in hospital in a coma.
A victim of society's neglect, he is later revealed
as a victimiser. The setting is a concrete, urban
rink, a nightmare world reflecting the grim and
soulless environment of the housing estate. In the
centre, a sewer-type recess becomes the
entrance for the actors depicting past events.
Around the stage, an arc of modern debris
provides props to tell the story. A sweeping
staircase leads upwards to nowhere. A huge
concrete wall cuts out the action from the past
and brings us forward in time, to the conclusion
of the play, where Roy meets his end. Behind this
wall the central panels are removed to expose
the edge of the sea as another reminder that
there is no way out.'

Director: Harry Gibson
Designer: Charles Cusick Smith
Lighting Designer: Chris Ellis

allusions to time

Marie-Jeanne Lecca

Salammbô / Philippe Fénelon

L'Opéra National de Paris
Opéra Bastille, Paris
May 1998 - world premiere

Above: Salammbô's dance

Marie-Jeanne Lecca: 'Based on Flaubert's 19th-century novel, the opera takes place in the ancient world of Carthage, full of mercenaries, priests and slaves. The music has a ritualistic, timeless character and this determined our decision not to anchor the piece visually in a specific time or place. Salammbô, the virgin, does her dance in her cold, lunar surroundings, watched by priests of the temple. Her first appearance is pure, fragile and ephemeral.

The transparent and irregularly pleated fabrics were deliberately chosen to create this effect, the image being counterbalanced by the copper and earthy colours of the mercenaries' world.'

Director: Francesca Zambello
Set Designer: Robert Israel
Costume Designer: Marie-Jeanne Lecca
Lighting Designer: Dominique Bruguière
Choreographer: Vivienne Newport
Conductor: Gary Bertini
Photographer: Eric Mahoudeau

*This image has been sponsored by
the Opéra National de Paris*

George Souglides

Cosi fan Tutte / Wolfgang Amadeus Mozart

Scottish Opera Go Round
Touring
September 1996

George Souglides: 'The night-time garden scene in Act 2 is a turning point in the opera. We wanted it to be sensual and sumptuous, but also chaotic and cluttered. The classical simplicity of the previous scenes is broken down and it becomes a garden of temptation and seduction.'

Director: James Robert Carson
Designer: George Souglides
Lighting Designer: Giuseppe di Orio

Executioner and Assistants
wind down blade

WHITE
NEON STRIP

MIRRORBLADE

EXPLOSIVE TRONG

[10] People clean off bloody
handprints.
NEON. lights up
sharpen blade [14] continues
Explosive flash.
Detatch blade ; Carry off ...
Leather patches on quilted shoulders.
Complete by [17] of 20 Amazons
— women —
SNOW STOPS ✳

Turandot / Giacomo Puccini

L'Opera National de Paris
Opéra Bastllle - Paris
September 1997

Top: Finale
Above left to right: Amazons,
Executioner's Assistant's, Emperor
Left: Storyboard Scene: Executioner and
Assistant's wind down blade
Previous page above: Outside the
Imperial Palace
Previous page below: The Tomb Room

Alison Chitty: 'Turandot was set within a
permanent metal structure with upper
level bridges, which were used by
Turandot's women soldiers for overhead
surveillance. The space changed with the
opening and closing of a huge pair of rear
doors and with the introduction and
movement of a double-sided wall.

The Bastille Opera has a very large stage
space and we decided to use it to its limits.
The grey box that surrounded the structure
was as far off-stage as possible and
lighting towers were in view within it. We
maintained a feeling of tension throughout
by limiting the palette to cool colours:
grey-blues, green-greys, charcoal and
gun-metal, punctuated by flashes of
blood-red. Only in the final image was the
world flooded with golden yellow.'

Director: Francesca Zambello
Designer: Alison Chitty
Lighting Designer: Domonique Bruguière
Choreographer: Alfonse Poulin
Photographer: Eric Mahoudeau

Andrew Wood

The Trial / Franz Kafka, adapted by
Stephen Berkoff

Contact Theatre Company
The Dancehouse - Manchester
April 1997

Act 1: Joseph K and voices

Andrew Wood: 'A harsh, angular landscape
developed from responses to the period and the
imagery of Kafka's original text. These were
distorted to incorporate the theatricality of the
production's locations. Timescales became fluid
and intertwined as the lighting, sound and
performers transformed the space, whilst
duplicating or responding to the course of
Joseph K's nightmare.'

Director: Gareth Tudor Price
Designer: Andrew Wood
Lighting Designer: Paul Colley
Photographer: Louise Adkins

Merle Hensel

Waiting for the Past / Devised by
Sabine Hausherr and Merle Hensel

Central Saint Martin's College of Art and Design
The Rivoli Ballroom - London
April 1998

Merle Hensel: 'This was a site-specific dance
production in which we aimed to capture the
atmosphere of this exceptional space and the
different perceptions and reality of time within it.
I developed the set and costumes along with the
concept, choreography and the characters
during improvisation and rehearsals. This way of
working allowed for a much greater connection
between all aspects of the piece.'

Director and Choreographers: Sabine Hausherr
and Merle Hensel
Design and Lighting: Merle Hensel
Photographer: Andrew Downes

time+space

Anna Fleischle

Krankheit der Jugend
Ferdinand Bruckner

Garage, Theater Erlangen - Germany
January 1998

Left: Act 3, scene 5
Below left: Alt and Desiree

Anna Fleischle: 'What was nominally a hostel for medical students evolved into a sterile, hermetic environment where pessimistic souls contemplated the nature of existence and its inevitable conclusion. The almost anti-space, lacking in definition and without personality, needed to reflect the disillusionment of the characters, to mirror the timelessness of their human dilemmas. The many doors, without clear destinations, encouraged transience and fluidity, compelling the characters to interact and strive for intimacy in that most oppressive of environments.'

Director: Celina Nicolay
Designer: Anna Fleischle
Lighting Designer: Gerd Budschigk
Dramaturg: Thomas Reher

Stanley / Pam Gems

Cottesloe Theatre
Royal National Theatre - London
January 1996

Tim Hatley: 'The artist Stanley Spencer dreamt of creating a cathedral full of his work. The design for Pam Gems' play attempted to fulfil his dream. The audience sat in church pews and his paintings in progress dominated the design around the entire auditorium.'

Director: John Caird
Designer: Tim Hatley
Lighting Designer: Peter Mumford

*This image has been sponsored
by Royal National Theatre*

Tim Hatley

allusions to time

Julietta / Bohuslav Martinu

Opera North and Opera Zuid, Holland
Grand Theatre - Leeds and touring
October 1997

Above: Michel arrives in a small coastal town, in search
of a beautiful girl he heard singing a long time ago
Right: Madame La Comtesse on the seafront

Stefanos Lazaridis: 'Julietta is a lost world of dreams
and nostalgia. Its inhabitants have a clear logic for each
moment, but they have long since lost the ability to
connect these moments together. The space plays with
that ambiguity, suggesting a beach, a hotel, a hospital:
locations of ephemeral meetings and poignant
departures. The vast window, which is also a mirror,
implies that the only view these disturbed psyches
possess is a distorted one of themselves, condemned
to wander in the limitless prison of the mind.

Marie-Jeanne Lecca: ' The costumes carry the
flavour of a pre-war, French, seaside resort in sun-
bleached colours, which retains an appearance of
normality in this uncertain borderland between dream
and reality.'

Director: David Pountney
Set Designer: Stefanos Lazaridis
Costume Designer: Marie-Jeanne Lecca
Lighting Designer: David Cunningham
Conductor: Steuart Bedford
Photographer: Clive Barda

These images have been sponsored by Opera North

The Turn of the Screw / Benjamin Britten and
Myfanwy Piper, after Henry James

Théâtre Royal de las Monnaie - Brussels
June 1998

Above: Act 2, scene 1

Stefanos Lazaridis: 'The governess: "Lost in
my labyrinth I see no truth, only the foggy walls of
evil press upon me. Lost in my labyrinth I see no
truth. O innocence, you have corrupted me,
which way shall I turn? I know nothing of evil, yet I
feel it, I fear it, worse - imagine it. Lost in my
labyrinth, which way shall I turn?"

1998 Opernwelt German Critics' Award -
Designer of the Year

Director: Keith Warner
Set Designer: Stefanos Lazaridis
Costume Designer: Marie-Jeanne Lecca
Lighting Designer: Davy Cunningham
Photographer: Vassilis Skopelitis

Kit Surrey

Bouncers - the remix / John Godber

Theatre Royal - York
November 1998

Kit Surrey: 'Very few pieces of theatre correspond to "real" time. In the course of a couple of hours, we can be taken on a journey that might encompass hours, days or years. Time can be contracted or extended, moments can be isolated, almost "out of time". In this design I needed to create a space that allowed for all of this with the minimal use of costumes and props. Lighting permitted a brutal steel set to shift swiftly from mood to mood; from harsh cold exterior to glamorous, if tacky, clubland; and to that same "pretend" world in the sad, critical light of day.'

Director: Damien Cruden
Designer: Kit Surrey
Lighting Designer: Richard Jones

Bryan Williams

Sanctus / Thom Strid, Richard Green and Jon Holtby

Northern Theatre Company
Studio 2 Theatre - Hull

Bryan Williams: 'This is a future time: post-industrial overload, a time of fear and claustrophobia amidst the ruins of a broken, mechanised urban landscape. A mist rises from the dank and spoiled ground; a light shines. The thin, artificial rays promise hope of faith and resurrection, but the Messiah is manufactured; no more than protons accelerated in a cathode tube; a vision of a young girl with a message of beauty and truth, entirely manipulated by those who hold the real power.'

Director: Richard F Green
Design and Lighting: Bryan Williams

This image has been sponsored by Northern Theatre Company

time+space

Spyros D Koskinas

Ein Spiel mit der Zauberflöte / Wolfgang Amadeus Mozart

Bochumer Symphoniker
Audi-Max der Ruhr-Universität Bochum · Germany
November 1996

Spyros D Koskinas: 'A play of love and passion at the moment when fun-games and real magic transpose time into music. In a vast stadium, seating 2,500, the sacred trials are played out on a board of snakes and ladders set out on the arena floor. The Magic Flute: is it a game? Do we know how to play? Can we learn from it? The audience chooses the numbers and the cast moves and follows the story.'

Director: Keith Warner
Designer: Spyros D Koskinas
Musical Director: Steven Sloane

Fiona Watt

Heritage / Nicola McCartney

Traverse Theatre - Edinburgh
October 1998

Fiona Watt: '*Heritage*: a brand burned in deep through skin of centuries, scarring forever the soul, the land, the memory, the future. 1914. Two Irish immigrant families from opposite sides of the religious divide struggle to carve out a living in the vastness of the Canadian prairies. Through the re-telling of stories of an almost forgotten, mythical Ireland, Michael and Sarah gradually fall in love. The shape of the set makes reference to the coffin ships of the previous century, whose heritage still has a hold over the present. The perspective in the planking suggests furrows in the land, heading towards the same horizon; the hope being that at some point in the future they must meet.'

Director: Philip Howard
Designer: Fiona Watt
Lighting Designer: Renny Robertson
Photographer: Al Anderson

Quilt - a Musical Celebration
Jim Morgan and Michael Stockler

Mountview Conservatoire
Mountview Theatre - London
September 1997

Dana Pinto

Dana Pinto: '*Quilt - a Musical Celebration* is a compelling study of stories about the Names Project Aids Memorial Quilt. The performance was facilitated by the creation of trucks, designed to represent the walls of attitudes towards Aids. There needed to be the sense that each individual built this space and that they all now exist together. The stage becomes filled with patches, until eventually the set becomes the whole quilt. The effect is like a photo-mosaic where each patch has meaning, but as we step back we see that it creates one voice.'

Director: Ian Good
Designer: Dana Pinto
Lighting Designer: Nicola Morton
Choreographer: Chris Hocking
Lyrics: Jim Morgan
Photographer: Camilla Watson

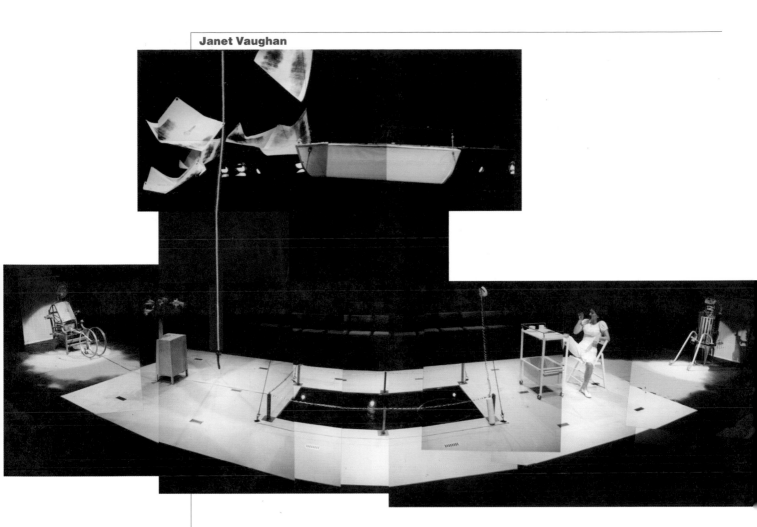

Smoke, Mirrors and the Art of Escapology
Devised by Talking Birds Theatre Company

Talking Birds Theatre Company
Arts Alive Studio, Belgrade Theatre - Coventry
June 1998

Janet Vaughan: '*Smoke, Mirrors and the Art of Escapology* was a site-specific piece telling, concurrently, the stories of two escapologists in two distinct times and spaces. Using all available vertical space, I created three layers: understage, the unseeen futuristic prison from which a prisoner attempts to escape, his story told through a soundscape and video projection; on stage, the sanatorium, where the wife of the escapologist Houdini attempts to recreate his (fictional) straight-jacketed jump through a hole in the ice; and finally, above stage, the place where the prisoner eventually disappears, up a rope, into thin air.'

Director: Nick Walker
Designer: Janet Vaughan
Lighting Designer: Bernie Howe
Composer: Derek Nisbet

This image has been sponsored by
Coventry Theatre Network

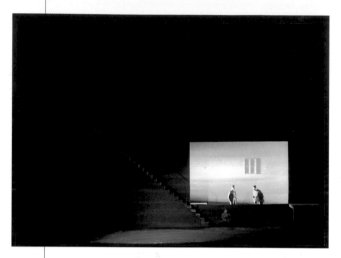

Katya Kabanova / Leos Janacek

Bayerische Staatsoper - Munich
March 1999

Stefanos Lazaridis: 'Katya is a story of the claustrophobic, provincial conformity centred on the family - outwardly stable and ordered, but inwardly riven with the contradictions which lead to her suicide. In death, she is subsumed into the river, the relentless and impassive force of nature, which is oblivious to the petty bourgeois drama. The ordered levels and strict compartmentalism of this society is presented as a series of boxes, oppressively cramped theatres of family life, which open up one by one to reveal their secrets. But in the last act, shorn of pretence, we see, as if in close-up, that this domestic structure is a ruin, perched on the brink of destruction.

Marie-Jeanne Lecca: 'The power with which the music depicts Katya's inner storm makes it almost unnecessary to attempt to give her and the other characters a concrete social identity, encouraging us to respond emotionally rather than factually. I tried to materialise the pictorial intensity of Janacek's music by creating Munch-like silhouettes: troubled and disturbing. Munch was not only contemporary with Janacek but very close to his work in feeling. Although the period element remains, the painterly look gives the costumes an abstract quality, almost baring them to an "anatomy of the soul" level.'

Director: David Pountney
Set Designer: Stefanos Lazaridis
Costume Designer: Marie-Jeanne Lecca
Textile Artist: Monika AlmeidaLighting Designer: Davy Cunningham
Conductor: Paul Daniel
Model photographer: Matthew Deely

La Traviata / Giuseppe Verdi

L'Opéra National de Paris
Opéra Bastille - Paris
December 1996

Ian MacNeil: 'We had just one hard and
sinuous object on stage throughout the evening –
seductive and threatening at the same time.
Perhaps it is inevitable that the escape to the
country will not be complete.'

Director: Jonathan Miller
Set Designer: Ian MacNeil
Costume Designer: Clare Mitchell
Lighting Designer: Rick Fisher

movement in time and space

Movement in performance occupies real time and space and yet abstracts gesture and form to conjure mood memories and memories in the body. Is there a direct interaction between dancers and scenic elements? This is now a basic consideration in designing for dance. Traditionally there has been little contact, but since dance is now made not only in theatres, but anywhere from art galleries to railway stations, the visual context can be inspiration in itself. Fine artists and fashion designers are often asked to design for dance. Their work exists in its own right alongside the choreography. They are engaged for what they do in another context. Is this connection with outside influences, this link to the real world in a highly stylised presentation, the frisson that provides the reason for taking or making dance in industrial or commercial spaces? If a dancer's principal concern is the potential of the body and the space around it, then the designer's role is to explore the creative potential of anything which could share that space and to extend, describe or simply embellish the body's astonishing abilities.

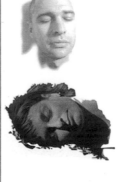

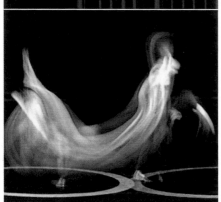

Eighty-Eight / Siobhan Davies
Conlon Nancarrow (music)

Siobhan Davies Dance Company
Touring
May 1998

David Buckland: '*Eighty-Eight* was danced to
the music of Conlon Nancarrow played live using
the original piano rolls. Ten dancers inhabit a
stage of industrial, stainless steel pipe-work
emitting steam, alongside six over-large pillows
imprinted with the sleeping faces of the dancers.
Lighting by Peter Mumford utilises twelve
Vari*Lites, which mechanically seek out dancers,
space and the design.'

Choreographer: Siobhan Davies
Designer: David Buckland
Lighting Designer: Peter Mumford

Swan Lake / Peter Ilitsch Tchaikovsky

Adventures in Motion Pictures
Sadler's Wells Theatre - London
November 1995

Rick Fisher: 'The eight white columns of the basic set were transformed by colour to reflect the location and enhance the mood of the dancing: deep blue for the joyfulness of the Prince's discovery of the swans and warm, more passionate colours for the third Act court dance. Pale side light enabled the dancers to be clearly picked out in this heavily coloured environment and with the addition of shadows from the footlights, the ballroom could become either frenetic or frightening. Later on the shadows from the footlights aided the drama of the swans' reappearance in the Prince's nightmare.'

Director and Choreographer: Matthew Bourne
Designer: Lez Brotherston
Lighting Designer: Rick Fisher
Photographers: Craig Shwartz and
Jay Thompson

The Protecting Veil / John Tavener

Birmingham Royal Ballet
Birmingham Hippodrome and touring
June 1998

Mark Jonathan / Ruari Murchison:
'*The Protecting Veil* is one of Tavener's best known works. He has said that he was trying to create the equivalent of an icon. In choreographing the piece, David Bintley aimed to create an icon in terms of movement. The work is played continuously but falls into eight sections, six representing events in the life of the Mother of God. A black box of austerity was constantly disturbed by the addition of celestial elements and symbols, rising heavenwards and falling earthwards. Upstage, a huge black curtain rose and fell to the stage floor, revealing a stylised gold-leaf wall or a black void, penetrated with light rays from above. Reinterpreting symbols in theatrical terms and using hidden sources of light, produced a spiritual atmosphere in which the dancers would appear to be lit incandescently echoing perhaps the quality of the ancient Orthodox church icons.'

Choreographer: David Bintley
Designer: Ruari Murchison
Lighting Designer: Mark Jonathan
Photographer: Bill Cooper

This image has been sponsored by Birmingham Royal Ballet

Arboreal - living in trees / after Italo Calvino

Scarabeus Theatre Company - open air event
Touring
May 1998

Muir: 'A free outdoor spectacle, which grows
into an elaborate performance of ominous stilt-
walking, woodcutters and flamenco dancers.
Performed at night with fireworks, abseiling and
climbing, actors wander their way through
Calvino's tree-clad world and reflect on the loss
of so much of our natural heritage. This work was
inspired by *The Baron in the Trees* and *Invisible
Cities* by Italo Calvino and by the Crocach
Crannah Reforestation Project'

Director: Daniela Essart
Movement: Claude Coldy
Set Designer: Muir
Costume Designer: Salvatore Forino
Lighting Designer: Lurca
Sparkled by: Les Sharp
Video: Gavin Lockhart
Photographer: Roger Bamber

Emma Donovan

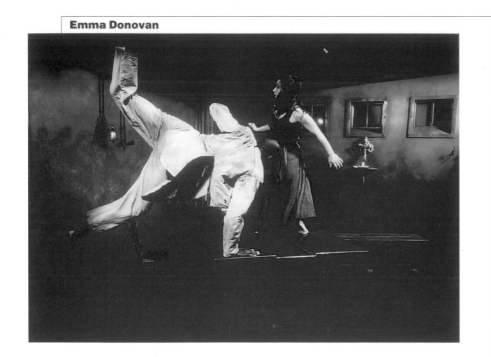

Miss Julie / August Strindberg

Derby Playhouse
May 1997

Emma Donovan: 'Miss Julie and Jean are forced to hide in his room from the peasant intruders - a decision, taken in a moment that has tragic consequences. To overcome the potential problems of interrupting such an emotionally driven play with a crowd of superfluous strangers, choreographer Louise Richards developed a short piece of fast, furious and erotic dance. Colliding with the set, the furniture, food, wine and each other, the dancers play out a sexually charged drama that mirrors the seduction taking place offstage between Jean and Miss Julie.'

Director: Laura Harvey
Designer: Emma Donovan
Lighting Designer: Emma Sainsbury
Choreographer: Louise Richards, Motionhouse Dance Theatre
Photographer: Chris Nash

Sarah Freeman

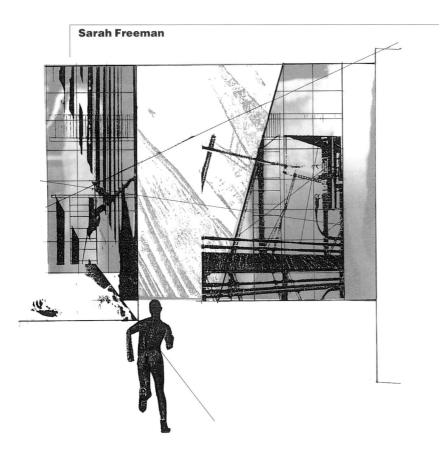

Mare / Sylvia Bazzarelli

Passo a Passo
Queen Elizabeth Hall - London
November 1995

Sarah Freeman: '*Mare* personifies the art of Capoeira with the story of a mechanic working in a cold industrial environment. The metallic backdrop opens to reveal his memories - a history of the development of Capoeira: from the sequence of a slave's ability to trick his master to the poetry of a sailing ship bringing dancing figures from Brazil across the sea to new worlds. The changing lighting and surface textures of the set relate to the fluctuating rhythm and emotion of this dance form.'

Choreographer: Sylvia Bazzarelli
Designer: Sarah Freeman
Lighting Designer: Paul Sadot

Gabriella Csanyi-Wills

A Chaotic Trip / Thornsten Knaub

The Indian Dance Company - touring
April 1998

Gabriella Csanyi-Wills: 'The Indian Dance Company required costumes which reflected and enhanced projected images, as well as ones that would refer to their ethnic origins and complement their particular brand of movement. The two pairs of dancers each had opposite rectangular sleeves which provided a large projection surface while dividing the space into sections. For the director and choreographer, it was an abstract piece, inspired by the startlingly beautiful and infinitely intricate fractals; for me it was like looking through a kaleidoscope with the figures moving through it, yet simultaneously being part of it, ever changing yct, at the same time, repeating and creating a cycle.'

Director and Choreographer: Rumana Omar
Costume Designer: Gabriella Csanyi-Wills
Lighting Designer: Thornsten Knaub
Projections: Rohini Kumar and Nell Breyer

Janey Gardiner

Connecting Vibes / Merceditas Valdes and Babatunda Olatunji (composers)

IRIE! Dance Theatre
Albany Empire - London and touring
October 1996

Janey Gardiner: '*Connecting Vibes* was a dance piece created by choreographer Beverly Glean using influences from Cuba and West African sculptural forms, particularly the Benin statues of Nigeria. Within this vibrant and earthy piece there were moments which were literally suspended in time; the dancers' bodies arriving at a sculptural form.'

Choreographer: Beverly Gleann
Designer: Janey Gardiner
Lighting Designer: Richard Moffet

movement in time and space

Sophie Jump

Trainstations
Devised by Seven Sisters Group

Seven Sisters Group
Kings Cross and Waterloo International - London
July 1998

Sophie Jump: 'There were two sections to this piece. Pictured left is the "platform piece", to do with the memories and hopes evoked by train stations. With high platform shoes and huge, billowing silk bags like wings, the three dancers progressed slowly up the platforms towards industrial wind machines. The "concourse piece" involved five dancers, dressed in suits, mingling with the passengers and emulating their waiting, greetings and farewells. It was interesting to watch the passengers and see at what point they noticed that something was different.'

Choreographer: Susanne Thomas
Set Designer: Ed King
Costume Designer: Sophie Jump
Photographer: Phoebe von Held

Rosemarie Cockayne

The Circle, a multi-cultural creation
Providence Row Users' Group

Providence Row Hostels for Homeless People - London
February 1998

Rosemarie Cockayne: 'The circle - an ancient symbol of unity. The circle dance - an ancient dance common to all countries. The users and residents of Providence Row Centres and Hostels for Homeless People in the City and East End of London come from many parts of the world, many streets and different spaces. They come to share food, warmth, accommodation and contact with staff, volunteers and friends. Some come simply to find a peace denied elsewhere. We each have our own inner space - our centre - and we each have our own inner time. True communication is infinite and timeless, filled with light.'

Director, Choreographer and
Designer: Rosemarie Cockayne
with participants in the project
Photographer: Photofusion - Crispin Hughes

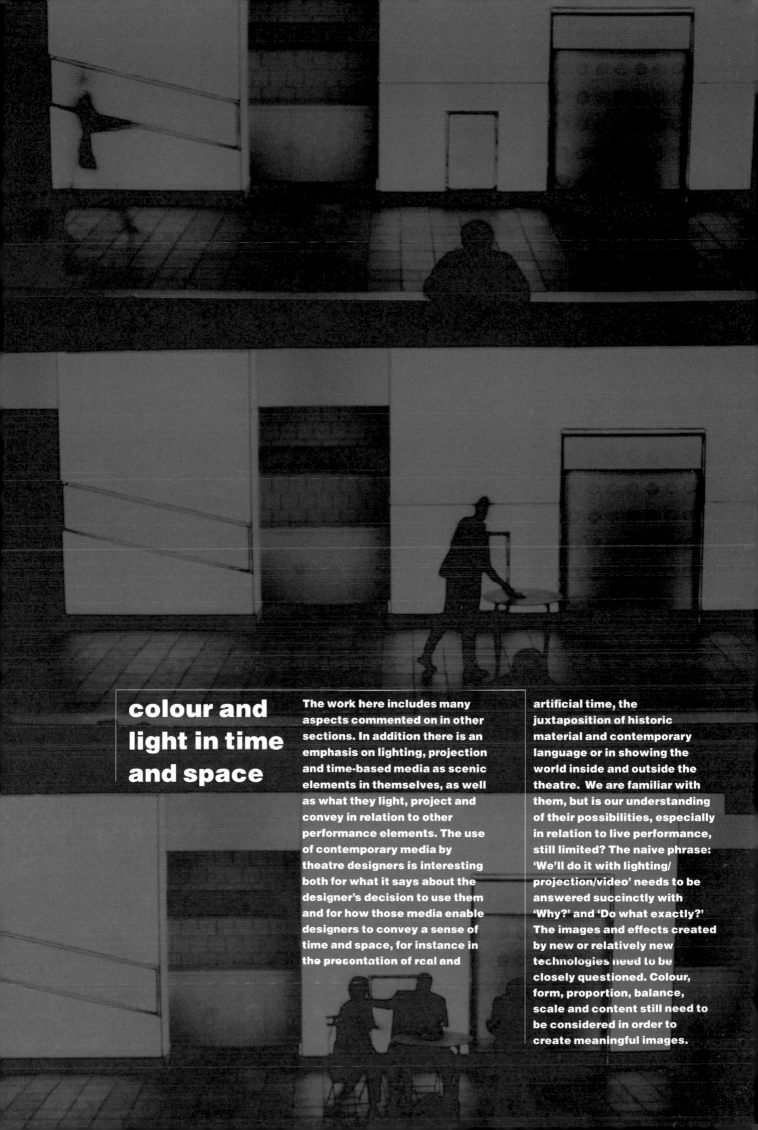

colour and light in time and space

The work here includes many aspects commented on in other sections. In addition there is an emphasis on lighting, projection and time-based media as scenic elements in themselves, as well as what they light, project and convey in relation to other performance elements. The use of contemporary media by theatre designers is interesting both for what it says about the designer's decision to use them and for how those media enable designers to convey a sense of time and space, for instance in the presentation of real and artificial time, the juxtaposition of historic material and contemporary language or in showing the world inside and outside the theatre. We are familiar with them, but is our understanding of their possibilities, especially in relation to live performance, still limited? The naive phrase: 'We'll do it with lighting/projection/video' needs to be answered succinctly with 'Why?' and 'Do what exactly?' The images and effects created by new or relatively new technologies need to be closely questioned. Colour, form, proportion, balance, scale and content still need to be considered in order to create meaningful images.

Love and Understanding / Joe Penhall

Bush Theatre - London and Long Wharf Theatre
Connecticut, USA
May 1997

Es Devlin: '*Love and Understanding* is a composition
of thirteen moments extracted from one summer in the
lives of two doctors and their visitor in west London
bars, beds, and hospitals. Scenes are cut together like
filmic frames. The chord between the final line of one
scene and the first line of the next has to be allowed to
resonate. The silhouetted choreography of the
characters reconfiguring their space is engineered to
effect a direct and pure transfer of energy from one
episode to the next.'

Director: Mike Bradwell
Designer: Es Devlin
Lighting Designer: Rick Fisher

Sadler's Wells Theatre
London
1998

Above and right: Auditorium side wall panels

Arts Team @ RHWL: 'A particular discipline of a dance theatre lies in the need for the audience to be able to see all four corners of a stage floor measuring 15 metres square. This infers a steeply raked, rectilinear auditorium. Inspired by the theatrical tradition of gauze that becomes transparent when back lit, we developed an inner surface of metal gauze panels which masks complex technical and adjustable acoustic installations. These side galleries can also be used for technical equipment or extra seating, in order to wrap the audience round the auditorium.

'Designers can extend their concept into the auditorium through colour, light and projected imagery, uniting the audience and performance. The principle of the panels extends to the tier fronts and ceilings to create a total concept. The balance between exposed technology and theatrical imagery is in the hands of the director and the designer.'

Architects: Arts Team @ RHWL
Theatre Consultant for Sadler's
Wells Trust Ltd: Ian Albery
Photographer: Nicholas Kane

David Cockayne

Carla Eve Amie

The Wall

Scenario: Theresa Heskins and Danni Parr

MAC
The Mayfair Suite - Birmingham
April 1998

David Cockayne: 'Designed for a hangar-like space in central Birmingham, the challenge was to create a physical and visual environment for this huge but intimate music theatre piece, with a community cast of seventy. An enormous catwalk was placed in the centre of the audience; the band was at one end and the wall at the other. Initial concern about the overall size of the stage disappeared as we saw how essential the performance environment was to such a large-scale piece.'

Arnim Friess: 'Multimedia? Theatre concerns all senses by definition. Projection for *The Wall* meant images of light, establishing scale and perspective. Live video moved us around an actor, into his mouth, close to his eye, away into an opposite corner. Still projection moved the whole space to the real walls of our lives and the imaginary ones of our minds.'

Directors: Theresa Heskins and Danni Parr
Set Designer: David Cockayne
Projection Designer: Arnim Friess
Lighting Designer: Jan P Sendor
Choreographer: Danny Price
Photographer: Arnim Friess

This image has been sponsored by MAC, Birmingham

The Tempest / William Shakespeare

Solent People's Theatre
Tour
November 1998

Left: Prospero, Miranda and Ariel (on video)

Carla Eve Amie: 'By projecting pre-filmed footage of the Court and manipulated digital images of Ariel, we created a collage effect where simultaneous events were viewed only by Prospero as a manifestation of his "storm of the mind". This use of video provided intense colour and depth in the space as well as reducing the on-stage doubling needed in a production with only four actors. However, the long rendering time of complex digital images, coupled with technical complications, tore chunks out of the rehearsal time. Our lack of sleep resulted in hallucinations as fantastic as any image created on computer.'

Director: Molly Guilfoyle
Designer: Carla Eve Amie
Lighting Designer: Jim Branston
Video Work: Graham Nye, Rob Thrush, Mary Swan and Richard McLaughlin

Simon Corder

One Canada Square - London
December 1996

St Mary's Church Spire - London
Islington International Festival
July 1996

Simon Corder: 'St Mary's spire (below left) was a pulsing beacon to the 1996 Islington International Festival, visible for miles around. A bright red lozenge. The top of One Canada Square (left) was lit to celebrate Christmas later in the same year. Visible from a great distance, it attracted considerable attention. These simple designs, topping off distinguished buildings for celebratory purposes; both address the big space of the sky. Seen from a distance, bright interventions into the night cause people to wonder and stare. Although separate commissions, I like the way the two projects sit well side by side, although architecturally separated by many generations.'

Lighting Designer: Simon Corder

Jonathan Cocker

The Turn of the Screw / Benjamin Britten and Myfanwy Piper, after Henry James

Pimlico Opera for Buxton Festival
Buxton Opera House
July 1995

Left: The tower - Quint's first appearance
Above: The gardens at Ely, at night

Jonathan Cocker: 'Rapid changes are effected by mood and lighting rather than extensive scene changes: from real to surreal and from the conscious to the suggested. Characters fixed in the real time of their costume and behaviour create a recognisable space, but exist in an abstract setting. A tight focus on a scene quickly changes to something more abstract, taking in the whole stage, less tangible - an alien space - the domain of the ghosts. There is a constant feeling of the interface between these two worlds and the anxious realisation of how the characters could slip unnoticed between them.'

Director and Designer: Jonathan Cocker
Lighting Designer and Photographer:
Ian Sommerville

Whale / David Holman

Harrogate Theatre
August 1998

Haibo Yu: 'When lit, the space behind the ice mountain symbolises another time and space - the deep ocean into which three whales are flown and the sea goddess Sedna wanders. The production requires numerous other spaces in different time periods, from an ancient Inuit house to a contemporary radio station, a Californian golf course, or a cemetery, to be invented and dissolved within seconds. The use of four triangular blocks allows for these demands to be met by actors arranging them on the ice floor, where and when required.'

Director: Chris Baldwin
Set Designer: Haibo Yu
Costume Designer: Tina Bicat
Lighting Designer: Paul Sheard
Composer: Paul Barker

Guy Hoare

No Fool Like an Old Fool / Neil Hisaud

Abacus Theatre Company
Pegasus Theatre - Oxford
April 1996

Guy Hoare: 'Colour was integral to the production. It transformed the floorcloth, transporting us to the different worlds of the three clowns around whom the piece revolved. Each had his own colour: cyan for Pierrot; magenta for Harlequin; orange for Coco. The choice of the colours reflected not only the clowns' costumes but also their characters - Pierrot's melancholy, Harlequin's vibrant surrealism and Coco's domestic warmth. The floor's colour reacted to the clowns' struggle for supremacy in their routines, but by the end of the play the personalities conflicted so much that the colours washed each other out to a bald white. The lighting reflected this breakdown of the comic relationships.'

Director: Rebecca Manson Jones
Designer: Jens Cole
Lighting Designer: Guy Hoare
Choreographer: Rebecca Manson Jones

biographies

Ali Allen and Marise Rose
Ali Allen and Marise Rose have been working together as a team for the past 12 years in theatre, opera, pantomime, carnival and on outdoor spectacular events. Their work has developed a distinctive style based on the idea that the design must not only produce a setting for a play, but must be integral to the concept and realisation of the production, changing and developing with the piece and transporting the audience from mundane reality to a visual world of the imagination.
They have explored the use of colour, texture and painting to create illusions of depth and space and also created sculptural structures which can be manipulated, combined or built together to transform the space. They have a 'hands on' approach, often carrying the design through to the final building and painting. They have worked with Opera North, Northern Ballet Theatre and Glyndebourne Opera; designed many touring sets for Major Road Theatre Company and Red Ladder Theatre Company and, for the past three years, pantomime sets for Wakefield Opera House. They also designed the lead floats for Bradford Festival (1992-97) and recently made a float for Peter Minshall's entry in the Trinidad Carnival. They have a long association with Pilot Theatre of which *Lord of the Flies* is the eleventh production they have designed.

Ian Albery
Ian Albery is Theatre Consultant for Sadler's Wells Trust Ltd. He has carried out feasibility studies and design for new theatres, opera houses and concert halls, restoration of period theatres and adaptation of cinemas and concert halls for stage performance. He has undertaken the preparation of architectural briefs, provided advice on audience/actor relationships, technical production requirements and equipment, administration, box office and catering. He has also prepared business plans for applications for National Lottery funding and has supervised theatre construction projects. Ian Albery is one of the founder members of both the Association of British Theatre Technicians (ABTT) and the Society of Theatre Consultants (STC). He has extensive experience in the UK and overseas in the planning, tendering and site supervision for the construction of new theatres and the refurbishing and re-equipping of old theatres. He is also experienced in planning law and other legislation affecting theatres, historic buildings and entertainment licensing. He is a contributor of data to the standard reference book on theatre design *Theatre Planning* published by the Architectural Press. Clients have included the Calouste Gulbenkian Foundation, Ticketmaster (UK) Ltd, the Scottish Arts Council and the London School of Economics.

Dawn Allsopp
Dawn Allsopp trained at the Bristol Old Vic Theatre School after taking a degree in Fashion and Textile Design. She is now resident designer at the Swan Theatre in Worcester where she has designed many of the main house productions over the past four years. These include *The Importance of Being Earnest, When I was a Girl I used to Scream and Shout, Macbeth, Second from Last in the Sack Race, Blue Remembered Hills* (co-production with Millstream Theatre Company), *Hard Times, The Malvern Widow, The Turn of the Screw* and *Mickey and Me* (community tour). Prior to joining the Swan Theatre, she was Assistant/Resident Designer at the Palace Theatre, Westcliffe-on-Sea. Designs include: *What the Butler Saw, M Butterfly, Up 'n' Under, Double Double, Dangerous Obsession, Your Money or Your Wife* and *Eye of the Storm* (Essex Young People's Theatre Consortium). As a freelance designer she has worked most notably for Snap Theatre Company, designing national tours of *The Borrowers, The Snowman, Snow Goose* and costumes for *Charlotte's Web*.

Carla Eve Amie
Carla Eve Amie graduated from Nottingham Polytechnic in 1991 and is a member of The Designers Formation. Designing for small- and middle-scale theatre and dance she has developed her passion for materials that reflect the emotional landscape of each production. Ranging from the mundane to the peculiar (and generally used in close audience proximity) these materials have included rubber, feathers, two hundred chrysanthemums, lead and plastic. Work includes: *Skinned* (Nuffield Theatre, Southampton); *A Room of My Own* (Hijinx Theatre company); *Iced* (Nottingham Playhouse and Black Theatre Cooperative); *Under The Bed* (Theatre Centre and Sherman Theatre, Cardiff); *Natural World* (Kali Theatre Company with Tara Arts); *The Tempest, Romeo and Juliet and Dead Rise* and *Tumble Home* (Solent People's Theatre). She lectures at Nottingham Trent University and has run workshops for Opera North, De Montfort University, Birmingham Royal Ballet and for the 1994-1997 tour of *Make Space!*

Luca Antonucci
Born in Venice, Luca Antonucci studied architecture in Genoa (BA, 1983) and then theatre design with Margaret Harris and Hayden Griffin on the theatre design course at Riverside Studios (1984-5). He was a finalist in the 1987 Linbury Prize for Stage Design and won the Opera Ascena (Switzerland) Theatre Design Prize in 1990.
Work in London includes: *L'école des femmes* (Shaw Theatre). In mainland Europe he has designed: *Barbarians* (Teatro Duse, Genoa); *La Bottega del Caffè* and *I Bugiardo* (Campo S Trovaso, Venice); *I due gemelli Veneziani* (Bergie Verezzi, Venice); *Lear* (Taormina Festival); *La Parigina* (La Versiliana Festival); *The Canterville Ghost* (Teatro della Tosse, Genoa).
For opera: *Ernani, Romeo et Juliette,* (Martina Franca); *Lear* (Taormina Festival); *Medea* (Verona); *Zazà* and *La Gazza Ladra* (Palermo); *La Parigina* (La Versiliana Festival); *Anna Bolena* (Bienne, Switzerland); *Le due Contesse* and *I due Baroni* (Casalmaggiore, Arezze). For dance: *Coppelia* (Reggio Emilia); and for film: *Nosferatu in Venice*; and assistant work on *Francesco, La Voce della Luna, Donna d'onore* and *Il Placido Don*. He designed an exhibition of the work of Emanuel Luzzati in Genoa (1996) and has taught architecture and theatre design with Luzzati in Genoa.

Arts Team @ RHWL architects
Arts Team is a group of architects and designers united by a passion for architecture to house the arts. It operates as a discrete entity within the RHWL Partnership. The team designs new theatres and arts centres or refurbishes and recreates theatres whose form no longer meets today's needs, creating new spaces and facilities and restoring those original features that are essential components of the spirit of place. They design concert halls, which gives them an in-depth understanding of the acoustic characteristics of different spaces. They also design music theatres, recording studios, regional and civic arts centres, drama and music workshops and performance spaces for schools and universities. Their work ranges from small-scale performance spaces, such as the Donmar Warehouse, the Auden Theatre at Gresham's School Norfolk, and the Arc at Stockton, to large-scale buildings such as Manchester's Bridgewater Hall, Sadler's Wells Theatre or the Lyceum Theatre, Sheffield. Staff range from those with well tried experience to innovative young designers. All have involvement in specific aspects of the arts. This serious commitment to the arts informs all the team's work and is a significant element of its success in building working relationships with clients.

Elizabeth Ascroft
Elizabeth Ascroft decided to become a theatre designer whilst attending her first summer course at the Manchester Youth Theatre. She studied design at Wimbledon School of Art and after graduating won an Arts Council bursary which took her to the Belgrade Theatre in Coventry where she designed *On Golden Pond, Golden Leaf Strutt, Sad Arthur's Trip* and *Agnes of God*. She has been designer in residence at the Liverpool Everyman designing *Trojan Women, 'Tis Pity She's a Whore, Love at a Loss, Wild Women* and *Man in the Moon*. Other work includes: *Macbeth, The Fosdyke Saga* and *Lie of the Land* (Theatre Royal Plymouth and Orchard Theatre); *Hard Times* and *Educating Rita* (Wolsey Theatre, Ipswich). As a freelance designer she has designed: *So Special* and *Fast Food* (Royal Exchange, Manchester); *Katherine Howard* (Chichester); *Give Me Your Answer Do* and *Apocalyptica* (Hampstead Theatre); *Death and the Maiden, Alice's Adventures in Wonderland, The Importance of Being Earnest, A Midsummer Night's Dream, The Three Musketeers, The Snow Queen, Kipling's Jungle Book Stories, The Comedy of Errors, The Winter's Tale* (costumes), *Robin Hood, Beauty and the Beast* and *Neville's Island* (all for the Duke's Playhouse, Lancaster); *The Grapes of Wrath* (RADA); *Zola's Earth* (Cheltenham Everyman); *Horror of Horrors, Pickwick* (costumes), *The Wizard of Oz* (costumes) (Northcott Theatre, Exeter); *Gargling with Jelly, Teechers, Bouncers, Happy Jack, Oliver!* and *Playing Away* (Hull Truck Theatre Co.); and *Holding the Reins* (Women's Theatre Group, London).

Elroy Ashmore
Elroy Ashmore studied design on the English National Opera Design Course. After a period assisting a string of eminent designers in opera, ballet and working at the Royal National Theatre, he headed design teams at various regional theatres. He now works as a freelance designer and is Head of Design for the Haymarket Theatre, Basingstoke. He has designed many touring productions and has created sets and costumes for theatres such as the Liverpool Playhouse, the Redgrave Theatre (Farnham), The Thorndyke Theatre (Leatherhead), The Mill at Sonning, The Royal Lyceum Theatre (Edinburgh), the King's Head and the Duke of York's (London). Work abroad includes: *Corpse* and *Ginn Game* in Hamburg; *Namouna* in Tokyo; *The Natives In Dreamland* (for the Louiseville Ballet) in Kentucky; and *Melodrame* in New Zealand and in South Africa. In Northern Ireland Elroy designed *Noises Off, Arms and the Man* and *The Tempest* (Lyric Theatre); *Aladdin* and *Little Red Riding Hood* (Arts Theatre); and all the Ulster Theatre pantomimes to date. Recent work includes: tours of *My Cousin Rachel, The Trouble with Old lovers, Fools Rush In* and *Aspects of Love* (Basingstoke); *Murderer* (Yvonne Arnaud Theatre, Guildford); and *All My Sons* (Liverpool Playhouse). A recent venture took him to Marbella and Paris to design major conferences for SmithKline Beecham and another to design the launch ceremony for the logo of Air 2000 at Gatwick Airport.

Austin-Smith:Lord
Austin-Smith:Lord is a multi-disciplinary practice offering services in architecture, interior design, masterplanning and urban and landscape design. The practice has an established reputation for delivering quality buildings that combine contemporary design with solid architectural integrity. This reputation is borne out by an award-winning portfolio which features museums, educational institutions, corporate facilities and historic conservation schemes. Their experience in the field of arts and entertainment features work at the Barbican Centre, the Lilian Baylis Studio Theatre for Sadler's Wells, the newly refurbished National Museum of Film, Television and Photography in Bradford and a programme of works at the Victoria & Albert and British Museums in London

Sue Ayers
Sue Ayers was educated at the Regent Street Polytechnic and then the Theatre Design Department of Central School of Art with Paul Colbeck, where she designed the opening production at the Jeanetta Cochrane Theatre. After five years as Resident Designer in Repertory at The Ashcroft Theatre in Croydon, she went to work with Bernard Miles at The Mermaid Theatre where she designed a number of productions in what was then a unique space before theatre became marooned in the 'middle of a road' system. In the early 1970 alongside freelance theatre work she began teaching part time in the Textile Department at Camberwell School of Art which opened another door to the world of art and design, the world of painting and the decorative arts. Whilst maintaining her professional interest in the theatre she has, along with Brian Elliott, formed Just Art, a fine and decorative arts group with which they exhibit every year. Work includes: painting tile panels, decorating screens and furniture, designing and publishing small books, building decorative pots and dishes and presenting small-scale performance pieces.

Mark Bailey
Mark Bailey designs for theatre and opera. He has worked for most of the leading British repertory companies and his work has been seen in the West End, across mainland Europe, in North America and also on BBC Television.

Martyn Bainbridge
Martyn Bainbridge's most recent theatre designs include: *Gaslight, The Norman Conquests* (Clwyd Theatr Cymru). Other theatre designs include: *A Little Night Music, The Birthday Party, Kes, My Cousin Rachel, Outside Edge, Pump Boys and Dinettes, Absurd Person Singular, Charley's Aunt, The Shadow of a Gunman, I Have Been Here Before* and the national tour of *Master Forger* (all for the Theatre Royal, Plymouth); *Measure for Measure* (Nye Theater Oslo, Norway); *Deathtrap* (Northcott Theatre, Exeter); *Outside Edge* (Churchill Theatre, Bromley); *The Soldier's Tale* (Oxford Playhouse); *On the Razzle* (Leeds Playhouse); *Intimate Exchanges* (Northcott Theatre, Exeter); *Brief Encounter* (Bill Kenwright tour).

Opera Designs include, most recently: *Ariadne auf Naxos* (Garsington Opera); *The Trial* (Collegiate Theatre, London); *Die Zauberflöte* (Kent Opera), *Madame Butterfly* (Phoenix Opera), *Norma* and *La Traviata* (Northem Ireland Opera), *La Rondine* (Royal Academy of Music), *Le Nozze di Figaro* (Guildhall), *Béatrice et Bénédict* (Indianapolis Opera). Martyn Bainbridge's ballet designs include *Daphnis et Chloé* for The Royal Ballet at Covent Garden. Martyn has also designed exhibitions these include: *The Astronomers* (London Planetarium); *Armada* 1588-1988 (National Maritime Museum, Greenwich); *Lawrence of Arabia* (National Portrait Gallery, London); *Daendels* (Rijksmuseum, Amsterdam). He also designed a major permanent exhibition for Madame Tussaud's in Amsterdam - *Madame Tussaud Scenerama*, and a new Chamber of Horrors for Madame Tussaud's in London. *The Explorers' Galleries* at The National Maritime Museum opens in 1999.

Keith Baker
Keith Baker read Drama and Theatre Studies at the Royal Holloway College, University of London, graduating in 1994. He then gained a postgraduate diploma in theatre design at Nottingham Trent University. He has worked extensively as a design assistant at a variety of venues. Design credits include: *Educating Rita, Night Must Fall, Who's Afraid of Virginia Woolf, More Talking Heads* and costumes for *Macbeth* (all Swan Theatre Worcester); and most recently *The Snow Lion*, a new play for children at the Polka Theatre in Wimbledon.

Hildegard Bechtler
Hildegard Bechtler was born in Stuttgart. She trained at Camberwell and Central St. Martin's Schools of Art. She made her opera debut with *Jacob Lenz* directed by Pièrre Audi at the Almeida Theatre where she has designed many productions.
In 1989 she started working with Deborah Warner for whom she designed *Electra* (Royal Shakespeare Company, Riverside Studios and Paris); *King Lear* (Royal National Theatre and world tour); *Hedda Gabler*, Olivier Award for Best Production 1992 (Abbey Theatre, Dublin and The Playhouse, London); *Footfalls* (Garrick Theatre, London); *Coriolanus* (Salzburg Festival); *Richard III*, French critics' Best Production 1996 (RNT and Paris); *The St Pancras Project* (London International Festival of Theatre); *The Doll's House* (Théâtre de L'Odéon, Paris); and the operas *Wozzeck* (Opera North) and *Don Giovanni* (Glyndebourne). Her frequent collaborator in opera is the director Tim Albery for whom she designed: *La Wally* (Bregenz Festival and Netherlands Opera); and sets for *Peter Grimes* (English National Opera and Munich Staatsoper); *Lohengrin* (ENO); *Don Carlos* (Opera North); *Simon Boccanegra* (Munich Staatsoper); *Mme Butterfly* (Opera Zuid); and with whom she is currently working on *Katya Kabanova* (Opera North). Most recently she has designed the sets for the award-winning production of *Paul Bunyan* (Royal Opera); *Les Dialogues des Carmelites* (1998 Saito Kinen Festival, Japan and Opéra de Paris,1999); and *Boris Godunov* (ENO) for Francesca Zambello. Her many film and television credits include: *Sacred Hearts, Business as Usual, Coming Up Roses, The Wasteland, Hedda Gabler* and *Richard II*.

Janet Bird
Janet Bird trained at Nottingham Trent University and graduated in 1996. Freelance theatre design work since then includes: *A Christmas Carol, La Cenerentola* and *Marat/Sade* (Nottingham's Next Stage); *The Iron Lake* (New Perspectives); *On No Account* (Candoco Dance Co./Visibility Festival '97); *The Beckett Season* (Etcetera Theatre); and as assistant designer for *The Family of Antigone* (Next Stage) and *The Swell* (Theatre Alibi). Installation design work includes: *The Hunt*, an exterior piece accompanying *Oh What a Lovely War* (RNT Mobile Theatre); and *Sideshow*, co-designed with Gary McCann at Nottingham Playhouse and Lyric Hammersmith for *The Cabinet of Doktor Caligari*. She is currently studying for an MA in Scenography at Wimbledon School of Art.

Rachel Blues
Rachel Blues trained at Edinburgh College of Art and the Bristol Old Vic Theatre School from where she graduated in 1994. Designs for the Swan Theatre, Worcester include: *Private Lives* and *Elsie and Norm's Macbeth*. For the Coliseum Theatre, Oldham: *Lucky Sods, Second from Last in the Sack Race*; costumes for *Alfie, the musical, Dead Funny, The Cemetery Club, Dancin' in the Street, Keeping Tom Nice, Brimstone and Treacle* and *Rebecca*.

Jan Bee Brown
Jan Bee Brown graduated from Central School of Art and design in 1987 and continued her apprenticeship at The Abbey Theatre, Dublin, where she became resident designer, designing *Purple Dust, The Glass Menagerie* and *Tagann Godot*. Her freelance work includes: *Hobson's Choice* (Derby Playhouse); *A Christmas Carol* (Theatr Clwyd); *Conversations with my Father* (Old Vic); *Montrose and Dead Funny* (Royal Lyceum Theatre, Edinburgh); *The Wizard of Oz* (Dundee Rep); *Piper's Cave* (Boilerhouse Company); *The Clearing* (Stella Quines tour); *Othello* (Tag Theatre Company tour). Jan was Resident Designer at the Stephen Joseph Theatre in the Round, 1993-1996, designing: *Forty Years On, Just Between Ourselves, Conversations with my Father, Oleanna, Musical Jigsaw Play, Haunting Julia, Gaslight, The End of the Food Chain, Penny Blue, Mr A's Amazing Maze Plays, Love off the Shelf, Physical Jerks, Cigarettes and Chocolate* and *Tomfoolery*.

Paul Brown
Paul was born in the Vale of Glamorgan, Wales. He trained under Margaret Harris. Theatre work includes productions for the Almeida, Royal Court, and Traverse theatres. Opera designs include : *Mitridate, The Midsummer Marriage* and *I Masnadieri* (Royal Opera); *King Arthur* (Chatelet and Royal Opera); *Lady Macbeth of Mtsensk* and *Moses und Aron* (Metropolitan Opera); *Parsifal* (Bastille Opera); *L'Incoronazione di Poppea* (Bologna); *Zemire e Azor* and *Tom Jones* (Drottningholm); *Lulu* and *Pelléas et Mélisande* (Glyndebourne); *Fidelio* (English National Opera); and *Don Carlos* (Sydney). Film work includes: costumes for *Angels and Insects*, and costume and production design for *VP at the Villa*.

David Buckland
David Buckland is a designer, artist and film-maker. He has designed both sets and costumes for over 20 works, mostly for contemporary dance companies, including Siobhan Davies Dance Company, Rambert Dance Company, London Contemporary Dance Theatre and Company Creange. Many of these designs have been for award-winning ballets. In 1988 he designed the set for *Eighty-Eight* (Siobhan Davies Dance Company) and revived his costume designs for the dance *Embarque* (Rambert). The designs for *The Art of Touch* were reworked for a film directed by Ross McGibbon and commissioned by the BBC. In 1999 he will design *Wild Air* for Siobhan Davies Dance Company and *A Stranger's Tale*, his first work for the Royal Ballet, choreographed by Siobhan Davies. His first solo exhibition at the National Portrait Gallery opened in March 1999. A book of this exhibition, cataloguing his performance portraits of famous actors and directors, was published in March.

Kate Burnett
Kate Burnett is a freelance designer and artist in education. Her most recent work includes: *The Little Mermaid* (Sheffield Crucible Studio); *Twelfth Night* (English Shakespeare Company); and Stavinsky's *The Soldier's Tale* (Hallé Orchestra Education department at the Bridgwater Hall, Manchester). She has also worked with Manchester schools on the 1998 and 1999 Manchester Arts Education Festivals, at the Forum Theatre, Wythenshaw. For the Royal National Theatre, she has designed: *Mother Courage and her Children* and *The Day After Tomorrow* (for 4-7 year olds) both for the Cottesloe Theatre and on tour. Other designs include: *Remembering Eden* a community opera with the BBC Philharmonic (Manchester); *B-Road Movie* (Lipservice); *In Search of Angels*, an epic community opera (Glyndebourne Festival Opera); *Doctor Faustus* - Time Out Award for Theatre Design (Young Vic); *Brighton Rock* (West Yorkshire Playhouse); *Of Mice and Men* and *The Threepenny Opera* (Birmingham Rep). She was head of design at Contact Theatre (winning the Manchester Evening News Design Award for an entire season's work in 1986-7). Her productions there included: *The Snowman* (also Leicester Haymarket), *The Little Prince, To Kill A Mocking Bird* (also Greenwich Theatre) Female Parts, *Mother Courage* and *The Duchess of Malfi*. From 1994-1998 Kate exhibited in and was the co-ordinator of the *Make SPACE!* exhibition of theatre design which opened in Manchester and visited galleries in Carlisle, Halifax, Sheffield, Brighton, Swansea, Brussels and Prague. The exhibition won the Gold Medal at the Prague Quadrennial in 1995. She is co-project leader for *Time + Space*.

David Burrows
David Burrows has collaborated principally with two directors for the last ten years: Phil Young and Alkis Kritikos. The productions designed for Phil Young include: *Crystal Clear* (Wyndham's Theatre), *Les Miroirs Brisés* (French Institute), *The Train Years* (MOMI); *Knickers* (Lyric Hammersmith); *Blood Brothers* (Heilbronn, Germany); and *Tonight: Lola Blau* (Old Red Lion, Islington). Work with director Alkis Kritikos has included: *Miss Julie* (Sir Richard Steel Theatre, London); *The Collector* (Portlands Playhouse, London); the British premiere of Beckett's *Rough* for Theatre 1 & 2 (Theatro Technis and national tour); *In Other Beasts the Best* (Theatro Technis); *Tartuffe* (National Theatre of Cyprus, Nicosia, 1997); and *The Frog and the Lion Fairy* (London Greek schools tour, 1998). He is a principal lecturer in the Theatre Department at Wimbledon School of Art (where he was trained under Richard Negri), and course leader of the Technical Arts Interpretation and Design courses. In the formative years of its development (1989-1994) he was also course leader of the country's first MA course in Theatre Design /Scenography. A detailed biography, many production photographs, costume designs and press reviews can be found on David Burrows' personal website which has been developed during the last few years and can be found at: *http://www.gangway.demon.co.uk*. The interest generated by designing the website has been the impetus behind the development of the interactive audio-visual project exhibited at the Time + Space exhibition.

Isabella Bywater
Isabella Bywater has worked extensively in both opera and theatre. Her Opera credits include: *Cavalleria Rusticana* and *I Pagliacci* (Stockholm Royal Opera House); *Ezio* (Théâtre des Champs Elysées, Paris); *L'Elisir D'Amore* directed by Stephen Medcalf (Victorian State Opera, West Australian Opera and Queensland Opera); *L'Incontro Improvviso* (Garsington Festival Opera); *La Belle Époque* (Sodran Theatre, Stockholm); *La Traviata*, directed by Stephen Medcalf and *Fidelio*, directed by Matthew Francis (Opera Northern Ireland); *The Marriage of Figaro* (English Touring Opera); and *The Masked Ball* (Opera de Monte Carlo). Other operas include: *Madame Butterfly, The Duenna, La Finta Giardiniera, The Marriage of Figaro, The Turn of the Screw* directed by Robert Carsen; *The Flying Dutchman* and *Eugene Onegin* directed by Nicholas Hytner and *King Arthur*. Recently she designed *Nabucco*, directed by Jonathan Miller (Opernhaus Zurich). Her theatre credits include: *Titus Andronicus*, directed by Deborah Warner (RSC); *Twelfth Night* (Royal Lyceum Edinburgh); *Of Mice and Men* (Nottingham Playhouse); *A Midsummer Night's Dream, The Tempest, All My Sons* and *A Doll's House* (Salisbury Playhouse); and *Hedda Gabler* directed Lindy Davies (Chichester Festival Theatre). She is currently working on *I Puritani* for Munich Opera, directed by Jonathan Miller.

Carr and Angier
Carr and Angier have worked on many prestige projects including: the Theatre Royal, Plymouth; St David's Hall, Cardiff; The Hong Kong Academy for Performing Arts; The Hong Kong International Convention Centre, Cardiff; West Yorkshire Playhouse; the Swan Theatre, High Wycombe; and Sadler's Wells Theatre. Currently the firm is working on the New Milton Keynes Theatre; re-planning the RSC theatres in Stratford-upon-Avon; the London Coliseum, (English National Opera); The Mayflower, Southampton; Snape Maltings and Cliffs Pavilion, Southend.

Robert Cheesmond
Robert Cheesmond graduated from Manchester University with a degree in drama in 1968. He now lectures at Hull University Drama Department, and is active as a freelance director and designer, most recently for a pantomime in a class B prison. He is a convenor of the Scenography Working Group of the International Federation for Theatre Research, and had given many papers on the aesthetics and politics of stage space.

Alison Chitty
Alison Chitty trained at St Martin's School of Art and at Central School of Art and Design in London. She went on to design over 40 productions at the New Victoria Theatre in North Staffordshire as well as *Uncle Vanya* (Hampstead Theatre); *Measure for Measure* and *Julius Caesar* (Riverside Studios); and *Carmen Jones* (Crucible Theatre, Sheffield and West End). Other designs include: *Tartuffe, Volpone,*

Breaking the Silence and *Romeo and Juliet* (Royal Shakespeare Company). She was resident Designer at the Royal National Theatre for eight years where her work included: *A Month in the Country, Don Juan, Much Ado About Nothing The Prince of Homburg, Danton's Death, Major Barbara, Kick for Touch, Venice Preserv'd* (British Drama Award), *Tales from Hollywood, Antigone* and *Fool for Love* (which transferred to the West End). She also designed Sir Peter Hall's productions of *Antony and Cleopatra, The Winter's Tale, Cymbeline* and *The Tempest*. Other work in the West End includes *Orpheus Descending* (Haymarket and Neil Simon Theater, Broadway) and The Rose Tattoo (Playhouse). She has designed many operas including: *The Marriage of Figaro* (Opera North); *New Year* (Houston and Glyndebourne); *Gawain, Arianna* and *The Bartered Bride* (Royal Opera); *L'Assedio di Calais* (Wexford Festival); *The Vanishing Bridegroom* (Opera Theatre, St Louis); *Falstaff* (Gotenburg Music Theatre, Sweden); *Jenufa* (Dallas Opera); *Billy Budd* (Geneva, Royal Opera - Laurence Olivier Award - and Paris); and *Blonde Eckbert* (Santa Fe Opera); the Olivier Award winning production of *Khovanshchina* (English National Opera); *Die Meistersinger* (Copenhagen); *Turandot* (Paris); *The Flying Dutchman* and *Julius Caesar* (Bordeaux); *Tristan und Isolde* (Seattle Opera). She is currently preparing *Otello* (Munich). Aida (Geneva) and *The Last Supper* (Berlin and Glyndebourne). Film work includes: *Blue Jean* (David Bowie Video); *Life is Sweet* (Mike Leigh); *Black Poppies* (BBC); *A Sense of History* (C4), *Naked* (Mike Leigh) and *Secrets and Lies* (Mike Leigh - Palme d'Or, Cannes). She is co-director of The Motley Theatre Design School.

David Cockayne
David Cockayne trained at Birmingham College of Art and Design. He has designed principally for regional theatres in Birmingham, Manchester, Liverpool, Leeds, Clwyd, Sheffield and Cheltenham. A substantial period in the seventies was spent in residence at Manchester Library Theatre, which he considers the best relationship between a designer and a theatre company. A production of *When the Actors Come* led to a continuing relationship with Don Taylor, the writer and director, for whom he has designed a national tour of *The Government Inspector* and Don's own plays: *The Daughters of Venice, Women of Athens* and *Retreat from Moscow*. Involved with theatre design education since 1980, he also works with the Society of British Theatre Designers, the Association of British Theatre Technicians and the Designers' Committee of British Actors' Equity Association. He is increasingly interested in music theatre and the spatial relationship of performers to audiences. He also works as photographer and visual artist.

Rosemarie Cockayne
Rosemarie Cockayne studied ballet in London and went on to the Royal Ballet Senior School. She became a soloist and then a ballerina with the Basle State Ballet. During her time as a ballerina in Switzerland, she started painting and was particularly drawn to the strong colours of the Expressionists. Returning to London Rosemarie both danced and painted, studying at St. Martin's School of Art. She decided to concentrate on painting rather than dancing, although she is enormously delighted when the two come together as in designing stage sets and costumes. Rosemarie has exhibited work internationally, from Clarges Gallery and the House of Commons in London, to Stockholm, Vancouver and Rio de Janeiro. She has worked in stage design, creating sets and costumes for *Nutcracker, Coppelia* and *Jazz Ballet*. Rosemarie's work ranges from pen and charcoal line-drawing to strong, expressionistic colour. She is particularly interested in taking art into the community and the environment and has been doing voluntary work with children, homeless and disabled people, hospitals and environmental groups. As well as sitting on various committees concerned with art and education, Rosemarie organised *Art with Children* at the Play Centre for St. Barnabas' and St. Philip's School in Kensington. Rosemarie is currently Artist in Residence with Providence Row, a voluntary agency working with homeless people in the City and East End. She organises and runs a variety of workshops in their drop-in centre and hostels for homeless people and refugees. This work has resulted in Christmas card designs sold for the benefit of the Providence Row Charity and an exhibition within a Flower Festival at the City's Guildhall.

Jonathan Cocker
Jonathan Cocker trained at the Guildhall School of Music and Drama and has worked extensively in the UK and overseas in both theatre and opera. Recent productions as designer-director include: *In Mozart's Eye* (MZT Dance Company at Spitalfields and Canterbury Festivals); *Don Giovanni* (Pimlico Opera on tour); *Mozart and Salieri* and *The Comedy on the Bridge* (Ryedale Festival); *Orfeo ed Euridice* (Northern Opera); *Dracula* (Opera West) and an acclaimed production of *The Turn of the Screw* (Buxton Festival). He has directed *Masquerade* (community and educational tour for Opera North); *Carmen* (Northern Opera); *The Fairy Queen* (English Bach Festival - seen at the Royal Opera House Covent Garden and the international Festivals of Valencia, Athens, Perelada and Granada). Jonathan has devised and run education workshops and projects for all age groups for Opera North, Opera 80, Edinburgh Festival and Nottingham Playhouse. For the Leinster Opera School in Dublin he has staged a number of student productions and has directed workshops on *Dido and Aeneas* in Melbourne, Australia.

Jens Cole
A former architectural interior designer, Jens Cole studied at Wimbledon School of Art and was a finalist in the 1995 Linbury Prize for Stage Design, exhibiting at the Royal National Theatre. Following a period freelancing, he was assistant designer with Northern Stage (an Arts Council of England bursary) at Newcastle Playhouse where he designed: *The Thief of Lives* (Newcastle Playhouse); *Hogwash* (Gulbenkian Studio); *We Would Like to Meet the Architects* (a performance installation in the Gulbenkian Studio); and a massive interactive performance installation *Adventures into the Unknown* (old Co-op building, Newcastle). Other design credits include: *Nightbus* (Birmingham Repertory Studio and tour); *Vortigern* (Bridewell Theatre); *Craig's Progress* (Mecklenburgh Opera at the Queen Elizabeth Hall and tour); *Tartuffe, Hecabe* and *The Trojan Women* (Oxford Playhouse); *The Tempest* and *Romeo and Juliet* (site-specific); *The Pigeon Banquet, Jack and the Beanstalk, Dick Whittington* and *Mother Goose* (Watermans Arts Centre); *My Fair Lady* (Richmond Theatre) and the double bill of *Play and The Ritual* with a visiting South African company (Riverside Studios). Recent architectural work has included the refurbishment and new offices at the Bridewell Theatre. Jens is also an artistic director of Theatre Present with which he has devised and designed two touring productions *No Fool like an Old Fool* and *Faustus in the Underworld*.

David Collis
David Collis originally trained as a potter/textile designer then joined the Motley Design Course in 1968. The following year he won an Arts Council Trainee Designer Award. He then became Associate Designer at the Royal Lyceum Theatre in Edinburgh (1970-3); Head of Design at Nottingham Playhouse (1973-8); Head of Design at English National Opera (1978-81); and has been freelance since 1982.

Sue Condie
Sue Condie trained at Nottingham Trent University in theatre design, graduating in 1992. Her first production, *The Canterbury Tales* (Edinburgh Festival) was awarded a 'Fringe First'. Since then her work has included: *Tongues Will Wag* (Greenwich Young People's Theatre); *Can't See the Wood for the Trees* (Roundabout TIE); *The Party* and *Stone Moon* (Theatr Iolo); and *The Legend of Pope Joan* (Liverpool Playhouse Studio). She has designed many projects for Action Transport Theatre including: *The Magic Book, Broken Angel* and an outdoor production of *Macbeth*. Sue was Associate Resident Designer at the New Victoria Theatre, Stoke for two years where designs included: *The Norman Conquests, Ghosts, Private Lives, Beauty and the Beast, The Hound of the Baskervilles, Overture, Oliver Twist, Aladdin* (costumes), and *Insignificance*. Most recently Sue has designed *Corpse* by Gerald Moon and *East is East* by Ayub Khan-Din, both for the Coliseum Theatre, Oldham.

Patrick Connellan
Patrick Connellan won the Linbury Prize for Stage Design in 1987 and has since worked extensively in theatre. Recent theatre designs include: *Paddy Irishman, Paddy Englishman and Paddy, Down Red Lane, Confidence, Julius Caesar, Pygmalion, Rough, The Atheist's Tragedy, Nervous Women, The Grapes of Wrath, The Pied Piper* and *Cider with Rosie* all directed by Anthony Clark (Birmingham Rep); *Top Girls* (Plymouth Theatre Royal and Salisbury Playhouse); *Coriolanus, When We are Married* and *The Rivals* (West Yorkshire Playhouse); *Limestone Cowboy, The Wedding, Neville's Island, Leader of the Pack, Silas Marner* and *She Stoops to Conquer* (Belgrade Theatre, Coventry); *I have been here Before, Twelfth Night* and *Macbeth* (Mercury Theatre, Colchester); *Time and the Conways* (Bolton Octagon); *Misery* (Leicester Haymarket); *A Passionate Woman* (New Vic, Stoke). Touring and West End productions include: *A Passionate Woman, Salad Days, Misery*, and *Conduct Unbecoming*. Patrick is an Associate Artist of the Belgrade Theatre, Coventry. He was one of the joint winners of the gold Medal at the 1995 International Prague Quadrennial exhibition with his designs for *The Atheist's Tragedy*.

Kandis Cook
Kandis Cook, a Canadian by birth, moved to the UK in 1974 where she trained at Motley (now The Motley Theatre Design School) having completed a BFA at Nova Scotia College of Art and Design. She designs for theatre, opera and ballet. Recently she has designed: *A Mad World My Masters*, directed by Sue Lefton (London's Shakespeare's Globe); and costumes for *Amor and Psyche*, choreographed by Kim Brandstrup, set designed by the Brothers Quay and with music by Kim Helvig (Royal Danish Ballet, Copenhagen). As co-founder of Post Operative Productions, in collaboration with Nick Till and Vocem, she has created a theatrical visualisation and sound experience of Monteverdi's madrigals entitled *Love and Desire*, commissioned by Tom Morris, Artistic Director of BAC, London. Their next collaboration, now in progress, is a theatre experience of the film *The Umbrellas of Cherbourg*. For Birmingham Royal Ballet she has recently designed sets and costumes for a piece called *Powder*, choreographed by Stanton Welch. Other work in progress includes: designing costumes for *Turn of the Screw* for choreographer William Tucket, set designed by Steve Scott, commissioned by Royal Ballet and premiering at Sadler's Wells; and sets and costumes for *Taiko* being choreographed by Stanton Welch and commissioned by San Francisco Ballet.

Simon Corder
Simon Corder joined the circus as a ringboy when he left school in 1978. He went on to learn his craft as a technician in touring theatre and opera. In 1981 he joined Lumiere & Son Theatre Company, lighting twenty or so theatre shows and site-specific performances in Britain and around the world. As a professional photographer in the mid-1980s he combined news and arts photography with original images for projection in performance. He has also designed lighting for the first night-time zoo in the world, *Night Safari* in Singapore. Since opening in 1994 over 3,000.000 people have visited this award-winning attraction. Meanwhile Simon's career as a theatrical lighting designer continues with over 100 designs for opera, theatre and dance in situations ranging from Europe's finest opera houses to studios of the avant-garde. Recent projects have included working with Operama on *Aida*, as projection designer with Patrick Watkinson, creating huge animated images for this stadium production. Other recent projects include lighting designs for The Royal National Theatre, The Featherstonehaughs, The Cholmondeleys, The Peter Hall Company, The Royal Court Theatre, The Young Vic Theatre, The Royal Shakespeare Company and Opera Theatre Company of Ireland.

Judith Croft
Judith Croft trained in fashion and textile design and then spent a year at the Bristol Old Vic Theatre School studying theatre design. She was Resident Designer at the Chester Gateway Theatre, then Head of Design at the Oldham Coliseum where she designed the first production of Dave Simpson's *The Railway Children* and Howard Goodall's musical *Girlfriends*. After a period of freelancing, Judith joined the Library Theatre Company in Manchester as Head of Design. Her work for the company includes designs for: *Ghosts, Two Way Mirror, My Night with Reg* (winner of the Manchester Evening News Award for best production of a play); and *Neville's Island* at the Forum Theatre. Musicals include *Goodnight Mr Tom, Company* and *Assassins* (winner of the Theatre Management Association Regional Theatre Award for best production of a musical). Judith takes great pleasure in working on productions for families: *Alice in Wonderland* (Heaton Park and touring); *The Tragical History Tour* around the city in Chester; *Peter Pan, Jungle Book* and *Aladdin* (Forum Theatre); and a series of Easter and Christmas shows at the Library Theatre including: *The Lion, the Witch and the*

Wardrobe, A Christmas Carol, Sleeping Beauty and the recent production of *Puss in Boots*. She has also designed the Neil Simon trilogy *Brighton Beach Memoirs, Biloxi Blues* and *Broadway Bound* and the Library Theatre Company's production of *Laughter on the 23rd Floor* (winner of the Manchester Evening News Award for best production of a play). The West End production, starring Gene Wilder, was nominated for an Olivier Award in 1997.

Gabriella Csanyi-Wills
Gabriella Csanyi-Wills continued working while studying with the Open University for degree in History of Art. She then trained at Central School of Speech and Drama in Theatre Studies, designing *Tango* (at the Kenneth More Theatre) as part of her course. She has since been working as a freelance designer. Recent work includes: Peter Shaffer's *The Royal Hunt of the Sun* with Lawrence Till (West Sussex County Youth Theatre); *A Dangerous Woman* with Fenella Fielding (New End Theatre); and the touring production of *The Mikado* with Jeff Clarke. Other designs include: costumes for *The Taming of the Shrew* (Cannizaro Park); both set and costumes for Room, *A Chaotic Trip, Recurrence, La Chunga, Joan*, an adaptation of Jean Anouilh's *The Lark, Between the Lines, One O'clock from the House, Amphitryon, All Manner of Means, Scapin's Tricks, Castle Spectre and If Mr Frollo Ever Finds Out*. She is currently working on dance costumes for Elizabeth Lea and studying for an opera degree on the Rose Bruford College distance learning course.

Anne Curry
Anne Curry has a degree in theatre design from the University of Central England. She has won a Royal Society of Arts travel bursary - then working in Italy - and the Sir Barry Jackson Memorial Scholarship. She continued post-graduate studies at the Slade followed by an Arts Council Design Bursary, working as a Resident Designer at the Oldham Coliseum (1983). Freelance work includes: *Dreams of San Francisco*, directed by Simon Stokes (Bush Theatre) which won the Thames TV Award for Best Play/Best Production (1987); *A Little Like Drowning* and *Winners and Losers* (Druid Theatre, Galway, 1989); and a variety of touring theatre. Recent work includes: *Half-way to Paradise* (The Drum, Plymouth, 1996); and *The Rise and Fall of Little Voice* (New Victoria Theatre, Stoke, 1996). Recent costume design work includes: *Listen to the Wind, Much Review about Nothing, Frankly Scarlet* and *Romeo and Juliet* (King's Head); *The Vivian Ellis Prize* (Her Majesty's Theatre) and *The Boys in the Band* (Aldwych).

Ann Curtis
Costume design work includes: *The Wars of the Roses* (1963), *The Histories Cycle* (1964), *Indians* and *Macbeth* (all in collaboration with John Bury); *The Government Inspector* and *The Romans* (Royal Shakespeare Company); *Moses und Aron, The Magic Flute* and *Troilus and Cressida* (Royal Opera House); *Don Carlos* and *A Night in Venice* (English National Opera); *A Midsummer Night's Dream* (Royal Opera, Copenhagen); *The Merchant, St Joan* and *The Beggar's Opera* (Birmingham Repertory Theatre); *Uncle Vanya* and *Man and Superman* (Haymarket Theatre, London); *Me and My Girl* (Haymarket Theatre, Leicester, also London, Broadway, UK and US tours) nominated for US Drama Desk and Tony Awards; *Owen Wingrave* (Glyndebourne Opera). For television: *Anthony and Cleopatra* and *Man and Superman*. For film: *A Midsummer Night's Dream*. In Canada work includes: *Twelfth Night, Virginia, Love for Love, King John, The Country Wife, Much Ado About Nothing* and *A Winter's Tale* (Stratford Festival); *Timon of Athens* and *The Club* (Grand Theatre, London, Ontario); *La Bête* and *Cyrano de Bergerac* (Citadel, Edmonton); *Albert Herring* and *Le nozze di Figaro* (Canadian Opera Company, Toronto); *Aspects of Love* (Toronto and US tour); *The Wars* (Film). On Broadway: *The Rothschilds* and *Jekyll and Hyde* (Tony Nomination).

Charles Cusick Smith
Charles Cusick Smith was born Glasgow. He studied at Glasgow School of Art and then post-graduate at the Slade School of Art 1979. He was awarded an Arts Council of Great Britain bursary for trainee designers with English National Ballet. He then became Associate Designer at the Library Theatre in Manchester, 1982-1986. Charles has been a freelance designer with all the major regional theatres in Britain. National tours include: *Ladies' Night, Hold Tight it's 60s Night, Hapgood,* and the national tour of *Marabou Stork Nightmares* adapted from Irvine Welsh's novel. He co-designed *Heavenly Bodies* a 1980s rock musical sequel to *Hot Stuff*. Charles also designed the costumes for *Rock around the Clock* for Granada Television and the Boyzone tour in October 1997. Other work includes: *A Picture of Dorian Gray* (Opera North community project); *Giselle* (English National Ballet); the rock ballet, *The Wall* (Opernhaus Halle, Germany); *Nabucco, Otello* and *La Traviata* (Opernfestspiele Heidenheim); *Romeo and Juliet* and *The Nutcracker* (Opera House Tallinn, Estonia). In 1993 he was awarded Best Designer by the Theatre Management Association for The Plough and The Stars (Leicester Haymarket), and Best Designer in the 1986 *Manchester Evening News* Awards. Charles is also a practising artist. He was an exhibitor in the Sunday Times watercolour competition 1996; The Royal Academy Summer Exhibition in 1997; The South West Royal Academy in 1997 and 1998; a one-man exhibition of paintings in Tallinn in February 1998, supported by the British Council in the Baltics and coinciding with the premiere of *Romeo and Juliet*; an exhibition of set and costume design at the Malvern Festival Theatre in October 1998. He is a member of the Cheltenham group of artists.

Es Devlin
Es Devlin trained at Bristol University and Motley Theatre Design Course. She won the Linbury Prize for Stage Design in 1995. Her designs for theatre include: *Betrayal* (RNT Lyttelton Theatre); *Yard Gal* (Royal Court Theatre Upstairs); *Piano* (Theatre Project Tokyo); *Love You Too* (Bush Theatre); *Love and Understanding* (Bush Theatre and Long Wharf Theatre, Connecticut); *Snake in the Grass* (Peter Hall Company at the Old Vic); *Hamlet* (Young Vic and Plymouth Theatre Royal) and *Edward II* (Octagon Theatre, Bolton). For opera her work includes: *Fidelio* (English Touring Opera) and *Don Giovanni* (British Youth Opera). Film production designs include: *A Tale of Two Heads* and *Beggar's Belief*. She designed *Four Scenes*, a ballet made by the Rambert Dance Company to open the new Sadlers Wells Theatre.

Robin Don
Robin Don's theatre credits include: Picasso's *Four Little Girls, The Marowitz Shakespeares, Sherlock's Last Case, Artaud at Rodez, Anatol* (Open Space); *Bartholomew Fair* (Round House); *When I was a Girl I used to Scream and Shout* (Whitehall, Bush, London and the Lyceum, Edinburgh); *Kiss of the Spiderwoman, The Marshalling Yard, Darwin's Flood* (The Bush); *Beautiful Thing* (The Bush, Donmar and Duke of York's); *The Water Engine, Spookhouse* (Hampstead, Vaudeville) and *Someone Who'll Watch over Me* (Booth Theatre, Broadway); *The Ticket of Leave Man* (RNT); *Twelfth Night*, and *Les Enfants du Paradis* (RSC); *A Walk in the Woods* (Comedy Theatre); *The Rocky Horror Show* (Piccadilly Theatre, 21st birthday tour and German tour); *The Winter Guest* (West Yorkshire Playhouse and Almeida Theatre); *The Knocky* (Royal Court Theatre Upstairs). Recent productions have included: *Fool for Love* (Donmar Warehouse); *The Shallow End* (Royal Court); *Cracked* (Hampstead Theatre); *Steaming* (Piccadilly Theatre); *Of Mice and Men* and *A Perfect Ganesh* (West Yorkshire Playhouse). He has also designed opera and ballet productions in London, Aldeburgh, New York, San Francisco, Lyon and Sydney. Robin's designs for *Eugene Onegin* at the Aldeburgh Festival were part of the British entry which won the Golden Triga at the 1979 Prague Quadrienalle. For *The Winter Guest* he won the 1995 TMA and Martini Rossi Regional Theatre Award for Best Designer. In 1996 he won Designer of the Year Award given by the London Critics Circle. Robin was production designer of the recent film of *The Winter Guest*.

Emma Donovan
Emma Donovan studied Theatre Design at Nottingham Polytechnic graduating in 1991 and won an Arts Council Bursary (for the Wolsey Theatre, Ipswich) in 1992. Colour and texture are recurrent themes in her work, exploring such materials as copper, lead, steel, earth, rubber and the media of video and projection in a semi-abstract design style in productions ranging from dance to new writing and classics, site specific work and tours of all sizes. Her theatre designs: *Desdemona* (Theatre Royal, Bath); *Andy and Edie* (Fireraisers Theatre Co. on tour); *'Tis pity She's a Whore* and *Miss Julie* (Derby Playhouse); *A Doll's House* and *Sleuth* (Salisbury Playhouse); *Twelfth Night, As You Like It* and *A Midsummer Night's Dream* (open-air, site-specific production for the Northcott Theatre, Exeter); *The Goodbye Girl* (E&B Productions on tour); *What Now Little Man* (Greenwich Theatre); *The Strange Passenger* (Paines Plough on tour); *Borders of Paradise* (Palace Theatre, Watford); *Road Movie* (Hull Truck); *Baby's Got Blue Eyes* (Theatr Clywd); *Macbeth and Winners* (Wolsey Theatre, Ipswich). Her designs for dance include: *Faking It* and *Twisted* (Motionhouse Dance Theatre Company). Film work includes: Art Director on *Paddington Station* (Paddington Station Films).

Liam Doona
Graduating with a BA in theatre design from Nottingham Trent University in 1986, Liam spent two years as a Design Assistant at Nottingham Playhouse before going on to work as a freelance theatre and exhibition designer. A number of museum and themed environments followed including: *The Tales of Robin Hood* and *The Lace Hall Museum* both in Nottingham
A lengthy instalment at Hull Truck Theatre Company, designing about twenty productions came next including several national tours and a number of new works by both John Godber and Gill Adams. Whilst at Hull Liam began working with director Damian Cruden and composer Chris Maidin a collaboration which continues and includes most recently a number of productions for the Theatre Royal, York including *Frankenstein, Habeus Corpus* and *Romeo and Juliet*. Other recent theatre work has included *Endgame, The Merchant of Venice, Krapp's Last Tape* and *Christmas Carol* for Compass Theatre with Neil Sissons. In addition to designing, Liam also teaches and is Head of Theatre Design at The University of Central England. The course has achieved notable success in recent years following its highly acclaimed work with Birmingham Royal Ballet and the establishment of its MA in Scenography.

Atlanta Duffy
Atlanta Duffy worked as a mural painter before training on the Motley Theatre Design Course. She was a finalist in the 1995 Linbury Prize for Stage Design and then went on to be Resident Assistant Designer to Rae Smith at the Lyric Theatre, Hammersmith for the 1996 season. Theatre work includes: *As You Like It* (Bristol Old Vic and West Yorkshire Playhouse); *The Farmer's Bride* (Stephen Joseph Theatre, Scarborough and tour); and *The Basset Table* (Bristol Old Vic and tour) - all directed by Poole Irvin with the Wild Iris Theatre Company; *Iphigenia* (Southwark Playhouse); *Rip Van Winkle* (Lawrence Batley Theatre, Huddersfield); *The Rivals* (Oxford Playhouse); *Angels and Demons* (Tricycle Theatre, London and tour); *Spring Awakening* (The Place Theatre, London); *Look Back in Anger* (Link Theatre, London); *The Swindler* (Pegasus Theatre, Oxford); and *In-between* (Cheltenham Literary Festival). Design for dance includes: *Instant Catastrophe, Tales in Motion, A Soldier's Tale* (Jointwork Dance Company); and *Woman Warrior* (Pegasus Theatre, Oxford). She has also designed Mozart's *Apollo and Hyacinth* for the Classical Opera Company (Britten Theatre, London).

Chris Dyer
Chris Dyer is an Honorary Associate Artist of the Royal Shakespeare Company. He is a Senior Lecturer in Design for Performance at Central Saint Martin's College of Art and Design and Director of Research for Virtual Stages. Although semi-retired, some shows never die; current productions include (1999): *Ines de Castro* by James McMillan (Scottish Opera); *Reineke Fuchs* by Goethe (Altonaer Theater, Hamburg) directed by Michael Bogdanov. Recent work includes: *Un Re in Ascolto* by Luciano *Berio* (Lyric Opera of Chicago); *Faust I & II* by Goethe in a translation by Howard Brenton and *Lord of the Flies* by William Golding, translated by Nigel Williams (both RSC). During the last year he took part in Choices in Gibraltar and Brooklyn, New York. *Choices* is an educational project for High School students developed by Tony Hill for the RSC. He was also part of a team that has drawn up a set of standards for CAD drawing in theatre, soon to be published by the ABTT.

Nettie Edwards
Nettie trained at Washington and Massachusetts before returning to Britain where she graduated from what was then Trent Polytechnic. She has since worked with companies producing a wide range of work - from touring in a suitcase to environmental promenade - and also in television. Residences include: Contact Theatre in Manchester (*Blood Wedding* won the Manchester Evening News award for best design); Head of Design at The Duke's Playhouse, Lancaster (where she designed their first promenade

production, *The Winter's Tale*); the Nuffield Theatre and The Everyman, Cheltenham where work included *The Sound of Music, The Pickwick Papers, Design for Living, Death* and *The Maiden, The Mayor of Casterbridge and Macbeth* (chosen as part of the Gold Medal Award winning British Entry in the 1995 Prague Quadrennial). More recent design work includes: *The Entertainer* and *Gentlemen Prefer Blondes* (Birmingham Repertory Theatre); *Not A Game For Boys* (The Royal Court and Derby Playhouse); Hereford's controversial community play, *The Visitor; Scary Antics* (Shysters Theatre Company at the Belgrade Studio, Coventry); *Twelfth Night* (Royal National Theatre's *Shakespeare Unplugged* project); and costumes for Terry Johnson's *Cleo, Camping, Emmanuelle and Dick* (Lyttelton Theatre at the Royal National Theatre). Nettie is also a freelance lecturer, researcher and painter, recent commissions include four large works for The Royal Caribbean fleet of cruise liners.

Philip Engleheart
Philip Engleheart studied mathematics at University College London and it was there, at the Bloomsbury Theatre, that he began his career as a designer. His credits include: *The Nose*, nominated for Best Design in the London Fringe Awards (Attic and Old Red Lion); *Rhinoceros* (Riverside Studios); *Friendly Feelings* (Quicksilver Theatre for Children at Leicester Haymarket); *La Locandiera* (Il Palchetto, Italy); *The School for Scandal, Animal Farm, A Slight Ache, The Singer, Fall Out Private Moyes* (Good Luck Company); *The Complete History of America* (Reduced Shakespeare Company); *The Bradshaws* (tour); *Stone* (Evreaux Festival); *Good* (Guildford School of Acting); *Amadeus* and *The Wizard of Oz* (Aberystwyth); *Scott* (inaugural production, Theatre Museum); *Aladdin* (Theatre Foundry), *A Woman of No Importance, Thirteenth Night* and *Rosencrantz and Guildernstern are Dead* (Bloomsbury Theatre).His interest in making good theatre for younger audiences has prompted such designs as: *Prospero's Children, All by my Own, One Hundred Million Footsteps, Baby Love* and *The Giant Prince* (Quicksilver Theatre for Children); *Story World, Summer Safari* and *Dick Whittington* (Theatre Venture); *Miss Fortune, East of the Sun, King of the Castle, Lifelines, Nightmare on Peer Group St., Anansi* and *Words* (Breakout). Most recent work includes: *The Other Shore* (Croydon Warehouse); *The Man Who Woke up in the Dark* (Trading Faces); *Poor Ted* (West Sussex Tour), *Weddings of Blood* (East Grinstead) and *Robin Hood* (Wilde Theatre, Bracknell). He also works as a director and writer.

Lis Evans
Lis Evans trained at Cardiff Art College and what was then Trent Polytechnic, graduating in 1987. She then went on to design, make props for and paint various productions, exhibitions and trade shows including: Circus Senso's Christmas Show (Hackney Empire); and *Equus* (Incompany Theatre). As Resident Designer at the New Victoria Theatre in Staffordshire she has designed sets and costumes for over thirty productions, most recently: *Kiss of the Spiderwoman, Translations, The Tempest, Aladdin, Return to the Forbidden Planet, Talking Heads* and a series of operas and operettas with Chris Monks including *Carmen, HMS Pinafore* and *The Mikado*. Next summer's quirky production (1999) will be *The Magic Flute*.

Paul Farnsworth
Paul Farnsworth trained in theatre design at Wimbledon School of Art. He has designed more than 20 productions for Chichester Festival Theatre's Minerva Studio including: *Summerfolk, Warrior, Love's Labours Lost, Translations, The Power and the Glory* and *A Midsummer Night's Dream*. Other designs include: *Volpone* and *The Merchant of Venice* (English Shakespeare Company); *My Father's House* (Birmingham Repertory Theatre); *Safe Sex* (Contact Theatre); *All's Well that Ends Well, The Taming of the Shrew, The Count of Monte Christo, Dead White Males* (Nuffield Theatre, Southampton); *Hedda Gabler, A Woman of No Importance, Sweeney Todd, Oleanna* and *Into the Woods* (Leicester Haymarket); *Transit of Venus* (Royal Shakespeare Company); *Make Way for Lucia* (Theatre of Comedy); and *Mrs Warren's Profession* (tour). For the West End, he has designed *The Cherry Orchard* (Aldwych); *Moby Dick* (Piccadilly); *Valentine's Day* (Gielgud); *70 Girls 70* (Vaudeville); *What a Performance* (Queen's); *The Mysterious Mr Love* (Comedy); *Edna the Spectacle* (Haymarket); *Scrooge* (Dominion, UK tour and Australia - Green Room Award nominations for both set and costume designs); and *Passion* (Queen's - 1997 Olivier Award nomination for Best Set Design). For the Open Air Theatre in Regent's Park, London he has designed *A Midsummer Night's Dream, The Fantasticks, Lady Be Good, A Connecticut Yankee, The Music Man, Kiss Me Kate, Gentlemen Prefer Blondes* and *Troilus and Cressida*. Recent work includes: *Hay Fever; A Flea in Her Ear; My Fair Lady* (Det Ny Teater, Copenhagen); *The Pirates of Penzance* (West Yorkshire Playhouse); and *A Tale of Two Cities* (tour).

Jonathan Fensom
Jonathan Fensom trained in Theatre Design at Nottingham Polytechnic. Recent theatre work includes: *Assassins* (national tour); *Dangerous Corner* and *The Government Inspector* (Watermill Theatre, Newbury); the Soho Season: 5 plays: 4 weeks (Pleasance London); *Richard III* (Pleasance London, Neuss, Oldenburg and Chemnitz, Germany); *Closer than Ever* (Jermyn Street Theatre); *Schippel The Plumber* (Palace Theatre, Watford); *Take Away* (Mu-lan Theatre Company); *Bouncers* (Mercury Theatre, Colchester); Ghetto (Riverside Studios); *Roots and Wings* and *An Evening with Gary Lineker* (Sherman Theatre, Cardiff); *A Nightingale Sang* (Nuffield Theatre, Southampton); *Yusupov* (Sydmonton Festival); *The Importance of Being Earnest, Wait Until Dark* and *Billy Liar* (Salisbury Playhouse); *September Tide* (King's Head, Thorndike Theatre, Leatherhead and Comedy Theatre, West End). Jonathan was Associate Designer on *The Lion King* (New Amsterdam Theatre, Broadway) and has worked as an assistant designer to Richard Hudson on many occasions. He has also led design workshops for the Royal National Theatre's Education Department.

Rick Fisher
Originally from the US, Rick Fisher has worked in British theatre for over 15 years and is currently Chairman of the Association of Lighting Designers. He won the 1998 Olivier Award for his lighting of *Lady in the Dark* and *Chips with Everything* at the Royal National Theatre. At the 1995 Prague Quadrennial exhibition he made a joint submission with Ian MacNeil of *An Inspector Calls* (Tony, Drama Desk Awards for the Broadway production; Ovation and Critics' Circle Awards for the Los Angeles production). He also collaborated with MacNeil on *Machinal* (Olivier Award 1994). Other credits include: *Swan Lake* (London and Broadway) and *Cinderella* (London and Los Angeles) both for Adventures in Motion Pictures; *Betrayal, Flight, Death of a Salesman, Blinded by the Sun, Fair Ladies Playing a Game of Poem Cards, The Designated Mourner, Under Milkwood, Pericles* and *Machinal* (all for the Royal National Theatre); and operas for English National Opera, Opera North, Bordeaux, Paris (the Bastille) and Florence. Upcoming projects include: *Via Dolorosa* on Broadway and the *Hunchback of Notre Dame* in Berlin.

Penny Fitt
Penny Fitt studied Theatre Design at Motley (1987-1988) and worked in London as a freelance designer for the next three years. In that time she designed over 30 pieces, mostly for theatre but with occasional work for dance and opera. Her designs include: *I Miss My War* (Almeida Theatre); *Street Scene* (ENO Baylis Programme and Brixton Prison); *Fools' Mate* (New End Theatre, Hampstead); and *Theresa* (Pascal Theatre Company at the Gulbenkian Studio Theatre, Newcastle and tour). In 1991 she moved to Manchester and became Resident Designer at the Octagon Theatre in Bolton designing, among other productions, *Blue Remembered Hills, The Norman Conquests, Feed, Death of a Salesman, Titus Andronicus* and *The Suicide*. She now lives in Bristol and has been running the Theatre Design Course at Bristol Old Vic Theatre School since 1996.

Anna Fleischle
Anna Fleischle was born in Munich and is now resident in Britain. She trained at Central Saint Martins College of Art and Design. Theatre credits include: *The Baa-Lamb's Holiday* (Theater K, Aachen, Germany); *Krankheit der Jugend, Allerleirauh, Twelfth Night* (costumes only) and *The Threepenny Opera*, costumes only (Theater Erlangen, Germany); *The Date* (Staines Old Town Hall Art Centre and Lillian Baylis Theatre); *An Inspector Calls* (Theater in der Leopoldstrasse, Munich); *Bodily Harm* (Cochrane Theatre). Work in film includes: *Fallen Boy/Dream City* (CSM and the HDK, Berlin); *Assault* (LCP, London for Fuji Competition 1995), and *Chronic Mind Topes* (television project for LCP, London). She also teaches assistant designers and apprentices at the Theater Erlangen in Germany.

Richard Foxton
Richard Foxton studied Theatre Design at Nottingham Trent Polytechnic. He has been the Resident Designer at the Octagon Theatre, Bolton since 1993, designing over 30 productions including: *Early One Morning, The Resurrectionists, Saved, Hysteria, Gaslight, Dancing at Lughnasa, Enjoy, Macbeth, A Midsummer Night's Dream, Blood Wedding, Under Milkwood, Happy Days, The Ghost Train, The Fastest Clock in the Universe* and *The Pitchfork Disney*. Other design work includes: *Dead Funny* (Salisbury Playhouse and Theatr Clwyd); *Kes, the musical* (Theatre Royal, York); *Kvech* (West Yorkshire Playhouse); *A Clockwork Orange* (TAG, Glasgow), *Man Equals Man, Oedipus Tyrannos* and *Woza Albert* (Contact Theatre, Manchester); and *Murderer Hope of Womankind* (Whitworth Art Gallery, Manchester). The design for *Murderer Hope of Womankind* was part of the gold medal winning British exhibit at the 1995 Prague Quadrennial. Richard has had seven nominations for the Manchester Evening News Design Award, winning twice in 1992 and 1994. In 1997 he served as a member of the judging panel for the Linbury Prize for Stage Design.

Sarah Freeman
Sarah Freeman has a BSc (Hons) in Architecture from the Bartlett School of Architecture (1993) and a Higher Diploma in Theatre Design from the Slade School of Fine Art (1996). Her work in theatre includes: props for productions of *The Beaux' Stratagem* and *The Changeling*; stage construction for *Uncle Vanya* (Questors' Theatre, 1994); set design for Strindberg's *Playing with Fire* directed by Sebastian Doggart (Redcube at the Theatre Museum, 1995); sets and costumes for *Mare* (Passo a Passo at Jackson's Lane Theatre, the Royal Festival Hall and the Queen Elizabeth Hall, 1995). She has participated in various architectural projects with ABA Architects and Murphy Davé Architects. She is currently working for Collett Zarzycki Architects and Interior Designers.

Jane Frere
Jane Frere lived and worked as an artist for several years in Greece before returning to the UK to specialise in scenography. She trained as Central Saint Martin's College of Art and Design and at the Slade, where she was awarded the Leslie Hurry Prize in 1992. She has worked extensively as a designer in Greece, including collaborations with the celebrated Greek scenographer Dionysis Fotopoulos. Previous work in Britain includes: *Adam and Eve* (The Gate, London); *Rob Roy* (Royal Lyceum Theatre); *Night Sky* (Theatre Workshop); and *The Jolly Beggars* (Cottier Theatre and Festival Theatre, Edinburgh). In 1994 she undertook a major theatre venue conversion project for the Edinburgh Fringe Festival. She is Principal of Jane Frere Stilt Promotions undertaking projects for a diverse range of blue chip companies including Marks and Spencer and Cameron Mackintosh Ltd. In 1995 she became the publicist for double Edinburgh Festival award-winning theatre company, Teatr Biuro Podrozy from Poland. In 1996 she produced the company's UK tour and has remained its international manager. Future projects include designing a millennium production of the Coventry Mysteries for Teatr Biuro Podrozy in collaboration with the Belgrade Theatre.

Arnim Friess
Arnim Friess has an MA in Scenography from the Birmingham Institute of Art and Design. He has worked on the fusion of lighting and projection design for mainly studio-scale projects. This is theatre for all senses, close to the audience. Stage work includes: Mozart's *Mass in C-Minor* (Birmingham Royal Ballet); *Brief History of Time - The Stage Show* (The Works); and *Hard Day's Night* (Hull Truck). He is also a trained photographer. Other work includes lighting exhibitions, an MTV video and a 360 degree audio-visual installation in Sheffield's The Republic.

Janey Gardiner
Janey Gardiner trained in theatre design at Central St Martins College of Art and Design where she now teaches the history of costume on a freelance basis. She was Associate Designer at the Redgrave Theatre Farnham, 1991-93, where productions included: *Comedy of Errors, Happy Family* and *Don't Rock The Boat*. Other regional repertory work has been with the Contact and Library Theatres in Manchester and most recently *Caravan* and *Elsie and Norm's Macbeth* for the

Liverpool Everyman Theatre. Touring work has included commissions from companies such as Eastern Angles and Black Theatre Co-op. Dance work has been with IRIE! Dance Theatre and Duende for Suraya Hilal at the Queen Elizabeth Hall. Work in drama schools includes designs for LAMDA, Guildford School of Acting and Central School of Speech and Drama. Janey is and has been a visiting lecturer on numerous design and drama courses.

Tim Goodchild
Tim Goodchild's theatre designs include: *The Taming of the Shrew*, *The Relapse*, *Xenobia*, *Three Hours After Marriage* and *The Merry Wives of Windsor* (RSC); *Wonderful Town*, *Killing Jessica*, *Cafe Puccini*, *Pump Boys and Dinettes*, *Little Shop of Horrors*, *Blondel*, *Oklahoma!*, *My Fair Lady*, *Hello Dolly*, *The Two Ronnies*, *Hans Andersen*, *Gone with the Wind*, *Phil The Flutter*, *Salad Days*, *Thomas and the King*, *Troubadour*, *Sing a Rude Song*, *Richard II*, *Hadrian VII*, *Colette*, *Cowardy Custard*, *Beyond Reasonable Doubt*, *Dry Rot*, *Switchback* and *Chapter* (all West End); over 20 productions for the New Shakespeare Company; *The Manchurian Candidate* (New Vic); *Five Guys Named Mo* (Lyric Theatre and Broadway); *The Corsican Brothers* (Abbey Theatre, Dublin); *Dead-Lock, A Slight Hangover, Towards Zero* and *Little Women* (Churchill Theatre, Bromley); *Enrico IV* and *Cinderella* (Theatre Royal, Plymouth); *Mrs Warren's Profession* and *Someone Like You* (Cambridge Theatre Co); *Bus Stop* (Palace Theatre, Watford); *Robert and Elizabeth, R loves J, Love for Love, Blithe Spirit* and *School for Scandal* (Chichester Festival Theatre); *Bless The Bride* (Sadler's Wells); *Buchanan, The Golden Years* and *The Three Sisters* (Birmingham Rep); *The Secret Garden* (The King's Head); *Dandy Dick* (Compass); *Look at Me When I'm Talking to You* (Leeds and West End); and *Brief Lives* and *Good Grief* (Yvonne Arnaud Theatre, Guildford). Overseas credits include: *The Bacchae* (Holland); *My Fair Lady, Tomfoolery* (Norway); *Antony and Cleopatra* (Egypt); *Peter Pan* (Canada); *Gigi* (Vienna); and *Oliver!* (Toronto). For ballet he has designed *Swan Lake* (Moscow Classical Ballet); *A Simple Man* (TV and Northern Ballet); and productions for Australian Ballet and Royal Winnipeg Ballet. Opera productions include: *La Traviata* (Royal Danish Opera and WNO); *Die Fledermaus, La Vie Parisienne* (ENO); *The Mikado* (Sydney Opera House); *HMS Pinafore, The Gondoliers* and *The Mikado* (Sadler's Wells); *The Tales of Hoffmann* (Victoria State Opera and Houston Grand Opera); *Cosi Fan Tutte* (Garsington Opera). Tim won the 1997 Olivier Award for Best Costume Design for his work on *The Relapse* and two 1998 Olivier Awards for Best Set and Best Costume Design on *Three Hours After Marriage* at the RSC.

Justine Gordon-Smith
Justine Gordon-Smith has been involved in making shows since her teens. Initially trained on the Technical Course of the old Royal Scottish Academy of Music and Drama in Glasgow (1985-1986) she worked mainly in production for site-specific performances. From 1991 - 1995 she took the Technical Arts Design Course at Wimbledon School of Art. Her recent freelance work in the theatre includes designs for *The Marriage of Figaro*, for Recreation Theatre Company (national tour); *The Great Feelgood Shagnasty Art Sting* with The Freakshow (Union Theatre, London); *Tales of a Bald Headed Boy* with Green Candle Dance Company (Islington Arts Festival); and

In Xanadu with Pete Brooks (Hoxton Hall). She has also collaborated with the award-winning comedian Bill Bailey on his video and many of his comedy shows, with Kristin Brunt.

Hayden Griffin
Hayden Griffin's career as stage designer spans over 30 years and includes many world premiere productions by writers such as Edward Bond, David Hare, Howard Brenton, Trevor Griffiths, David Mamet and John Osborne. He has designed 21 productions for the Royal National Theatre (eight world premieres), productions for the Royal Shakespeare Company, Royal Opera House (opera and ballet), English National Opera, Birmingham Royal Ballet and West End theatres. He has worked extensively around the world, including New York, Los Angeles, Australia, Yugoslavia, Canada, Germany, Holland and Italy. Hayden's feature film design credits include: *Wetherby, Painted Angels* and *Conquest*.

Peter Halbsgut
Peter Halbsgut was born in Werdohl, West Germany. He trained as an electrician and began his career touring Europe with various rock bands. In 1977 he joined the Frankfurt opera to work with renowned lighting director, Erich Falk, eventually becoming Lighting Director himself. Lighting design work includes: *Al gran sole...* (Edinburgh Festival and Stadsschouwburg, Amsterdam); *Die Entführung aus dem Serail* (Stadsschouwburg Amsterdam); *Otello* and *Cosi fan Tutte* (Jerusalem Opera); *Tosca* (Opera de Montpellier); *Die Geschichte von Soldaten* (Walkenried Monastery); *Aufstieg und Fall der Stadt Mahogonny* (Leipzig Opera); *A Midsummer Night's Dream* (Tel Aviv Opera); *Rossini Festival* (Frankfurt). In 1993 he became Lighting Director of the Bavarian State Opera in Munich. He was co-lighting designer for *Venus and Adonis* (Teatro Carlo Felice, Genoa and Nationaltheater Mannheim).

Tim Hatley
Tim Hatley trained at Central Saint Martins College of Art and Design and was awarded the Linbury Prize for Stage Design Commission in 1989. Theatre credits include: *Flight, Antony and Cleopatra, Sleep with Me, The Caucasian Chalk Circle, Out of a House Walked a Man, Stanley* - 1997 Olivier Award for Design (all Royal National Theatre); *Richard III, Goodnight Children Everywhere, Talk of the City* (RSC); *Suddenly Last Summer* (West End); *The Three Lives of Lucie Cabrol* (Theatre de Complicite); *Happy Days* (Gate Theatre, Dublin, Almeida and New York); *The Maids* (Donmar); *The Nose, Fool and his Money* (Nottingham); *Moscow Stations* (West End and New York); *Mr Puntilla and his man Matti, The Play about the Baby, Chatsky* (Almeida); *Damned for Despair* - Time Out Design Award (The Gate, Notting Hill). Opera: *Carmen, Orpheus in the Underworld, The Return of Ulysses* (opera North); *Les Miserables, Andrea Chénier* (Karlstad, Sweden); *Il Trovatore, Ariadne auf Naxos* and *Le Bourgeois Gentilhomme* (Scottish Opera); *HMS Pinafore, Die Fledermaus* (D'Oyly Carte). Dance: *Unrequited Moments* (English National Ballet); *Roughcut* (Rambert Dance); *Cinderella* (Northern Ballet Theatre).

Michael E Hall
Michael E Hall's earliest involvement with theatre was through his parents' magic act. Whilst studying for an engineering degree he became involved in student drama productions.

Work as an electrician at the Citizens' Theatre and the Half Moon led to his interest in lighting. Early work at Theatre Royal in York includes: *Kiss of the Spider Woman, It's a Girl* and *Romeo and Juliet*. He then went to Lancaster where he lit *Tis 'Pity She's a Whore, Bring Down the Sun* and outdoor promenade productions of *The Tempest, Much Ado About Nothing, The Tales of King Arthur* and *The Wind in The Willows*. For Cheltenham Everyman he has lit many productions including *The Mayor of Casterbridge, The Pickwick Papers, Amadeus, Annie, The Sound of Music, Blue Remembered Hills, Death and the Maiden, Dracula, Whistle Down the Wind, Lady Macbeth* and *Macbeth* (chosen as part of the British Gold Medal winning entry to the Prague Quadrennial 1995). Recent freelance work includes: *She Knows You Know* (West Yorkshire Playhouse); *Gaslight* (Bolton Octagon); *Coffee House Exchange* (Amadeus Centre, London); *King Lear* (Irish Tour); *All Together Now* (MAC, Birmingham); *Second From Last in the Sack Race* (Harrogate Theatre); *Love off the Shelf* (Harrogate and Nuffield Theatre, Southampton); *Scary Antics* (Shysters Theatre Company at the Belgrade Studio, Coventry); and *The Visitor*, a community play at Herefordshire Hall.

Peter Ruthven Hall
Peter Ruthven Hall originally trained as an architect. He now works as a stage designer and theatre consultant. He has worked extensively in opera both in the UK and elsewhere in Europe - Royal Danish Opera, Stadttheater Aachen, Opera Ireland (Eire), Opera Northern Ireland, Vienna Kammeroper - and has built up an extensive body of work at the Royal Northern College of Music. Opera productions extend from repertory works - *La Bohème, Le Nozze di Figaro, Madama Butterfly* - to a host of rare operas, many of them premiere performances: Cilea's *L'Arlesiana*, Delibes' *Lakmé*, Donizetti's *Roberto Devereux*, Lortzing's *Zar und Zimmermann*, Mendelssohn's *Camacho's Wedding*, Millöcker's *Der Bettelstudent* and Schubert's *Fierrabras*.In musical theatre he has designed original workshop productions of Andrew Lloyd Webber's *Sunset Boulevard* (Sydmonton Festival), *Tutankhamun* (Imagination) and *World Café* (Edinburgh Festival); and in theatre: *Love! Valour! Compassion!* (European premiere at the Library Theatre, Manchester), *Long Day's Journey into Night* (Theatre Royal, Plymouth and the Young Vic, London), *The Grapes of Wrath* (Crucible Theatre, Sheffield), *Women of Troy* and *Vassa Zheleznova* (Gate Theatre, London) and *The House of Bernarda Alba* (Oxford Playhouse). For the leading international design group, Imagination, his work includes the sets for *Joy to the World* at the Royal Albert Hall (in four consecutive years) which was also broadcast on BBC1. Peter was one of the award-winning British designers exhibiting at the 1995 international Prague Quadrennial exhibition of stage design. He is Secretary of the Society of British Theatre Designers and joint author and organiser for the national touring exhibition and book of British stage design - *Make SPACE!* and also for *Time + Space*.

Ken Harrison
Ken Harrison trained with Motley at the Riverside Studios. In 1984 he won an Arts Council Designer's Bursary to work at the Palace Theatre, Watford. He has since worked as Head of Design at the Mercury Theatre, Colchester and as Associate Designer at Pitlochry Festival Theatre. Other theatre work includes:

productions for The Lyric Theatre, Belfast; Druid Theatre, Galway; Theatre Royal, York; New Vic Theatre, Stoke-on-Trent; Tyne Theatre, Newcastle-upon-Tyne; Dundee Rep; King's Theatres in Edinburgh and Glasgow; Riverside Studios and Unicorn Theatre for Children, London. Tim Hatley trained at Central Saint Martins College of Art and Design and was awarded the Linbury Prize for Stage Design Commission in 1989. Theatre credits include: *Flight, Antony and Cleopatra, Sleep with Me, The Caucasian Chalk Circle, Out of a House Walked a Man, Stanley* - 1997 Olivier Award for Design (all Royal National Theatre); *Richard III, Goodnight Children Everywhere, Talk of the City* (RSC); *Suddenly Last Summer* (West End); *The Three Lives of Lucie Cabrol* (Theatre de Complicite); *Happy Days* (Gate Theatre, Dublin, Almeida and New York); *The Maids* (Donmar); *The Nose, and Fool and his Money* (Nottingham); *Moscow Stations* (West End and New York); *Mr Puntilla and his Man Matti, The Play About the Baby, Chatsky* (Almeida); *Damned for Despair* - Time Out Design Award (The Gate, Notting Hill). For opera he has designed *Carmen, Orpheus in the Underworld, The Return of Ulysses* (Opera North); *Les Miserables, Andrea Chénier* (Karlstad, Sweden); *Il Trovatore, Ariadne auf Naxos* and *Le Bourgeois Gentilhomme* (Scottish Opera); *HMS Pinafore, Die Fledermaus* (D'Oyly Carte). His designs for dance include: *Unrequited Moments* (English National Ballet); *Roughcut* (Rambert Dance); *Cinderella* (Northern Ballet Theatre).

Becky Hawkins
Becky Hawkins graduated from Goldsmith's College, University of London in 1990 with a BA Hons in English and Drama. She went on to study theatre design at the Bristol Old Vic Theatre School and has been a freelance set and costume designer ever since. Working with and for young people has been a particular passion and many of Becky's shows are for youth theatre and theatre in education companies. Designs include: *Korczak* (The Drum, Plymouth and Polish tour); *The Hot Rock* (Theatre Royal, Plymouth); *The Threepenny Opera, Oh What a Lovely War!, Sweeney Todd, The Hired Man* (The Drum, Plymouth); *Sylvia Plath: a dramatic portrait* (Contact Youth Theatre, Manchester); *Starchild* (Queen's Theatre, Barnstaple); *Can We Afford the Doctor?* (Age Exchange Theatre Company); *Into the Woods, Blood Wedding* and *The Visit* (Salisbury Playhouse); *The Rime of the Ancient Mariner, Shriek-Arena* (Salisbury summer schools); *Macbeth* and *Custer's Last Stand* (TiE tours, Salisbury Playhouse Education); *New Writing Showcase* (Ustinov Studio, bath); *The Hobbit* (Theatre Royal, Bath); *Bouncers* and *The Wind in the Willows* (Northcott Theatre, Exeter).

Marjoke Henrichs
Born in Holland, Marjoke Henrichs works as a theatre designer and painter. She studied art and textile art and then theatre design, at postgraduate level, at the Jan van Eyk Academy in Maastricht and with Margaret Harris at the Motley Theatre Design Course in London. She won an Arts Council Designers' Bursary in 1988 which resulted in her working for a season at the Royal Lyceum Theatre in Edinburgh. She was Associate Designer at the Wolsey Theatre in Ipswich from 1991-3. She took part in the British entry for the 1995 Prague Quadrennial, which was awarded a special Gold Medal. Designs include: *Romeo and Juliet* (Dukes Playhouse, Lancaster); *The Madman of the Balconies* (The Gate, Notting Hill); *Our Day Out, A Doll's*

House, View from the Bridge, Candida, Absent Friends, The Nose, Once in a While the Odd Thing Happens, Key for Two and *See how They Run* (Wolsey Theatre, Ipswich); *A Family Affair* and *The House of Bernarda Alba* (Royal Lyceum Theatre, Edinburgh) *The Wind in the Willows* (national tour); *The Importance of being Earnest* (Century Theatre, Crewe); *Long to Rain Over Us* (Leicester Haymarket); *De Troefkaart and Arcadia* (Haarlems Toneel). She was production designer for the short film, *A Paltry Thing*. Marjoke exhibited in the *Make Space!* design exhibition in Manchester (1994), at PQ'95, the *Make Space!* national tour (1995-8) and at the Theatre Museum. Her paintings were shown at the Summer Exhibition of the John Russel Gallery in Ipswich and more recently at the Halesworth Art Gallery, Suffolk.

Merle Hensel
Merle Hensel's extensive theatre design studies consist of a BA at Central St Martins College of Art and Design and an MFA at the Slade School of Fine Art, from which she graduated in 1998. She has collaborated with the choreographer Sabine Hausherr on two dance pieces, the first of which, *Together We Are Divided*, was performed at the Cochrane Theatre as part of Central St Martins Design for Dance programme. The most recent collaboration, Waiting for the Past, was a site-specific dance performance. Parallel to her studies she has designed and built the set for *The Date* (Blue Motif Mime Company, touring England); designed *The Whites of Their Eyes* (Fuji-Film) and worked for Tim Hatley on *The Caucasian Chalk Circle* (Theatre de Complicite at the Royal National Theatre) and The Italian Girl in Algiers (ENO). Since graduating Merle has designed a brochure for Hoyer & Schindele Architects, Berlin and is currently working on a landscape gardening design for the same firm.

Tim Heywood
Tim Heywood has designed costumes for the West End productions *Easy Virtue* (Garrick); *Artist Descending A Staircase* (Duke of York's); *The Boys Next Door* (Comedy); Elegies for *Angels, Punks and Raging Queens* (Criterion); *Spread A Little Happiness* (Whitehall); *The Dumb Waiter, A Kind of Alaska* and *The Room* (Haymarket). National tours include: *Steel Magnolias, Oklahoma!, She Stoops to Conquer* and *A Slice of Saturday Night*. Other productions include: *Whoop Dee Doo, Hedda Gabler, Under Their Hats, You Can't Take It With You* and *Flare Path* (The King's Head); *Guys and Dolls* (Library Theatre, Manchester); *Much Ado About Nothing, She Stoops to Conquer* (Northcott Theatre, Exeter); *Misalliance* and *Run For Your Wife* (English Speaking Theatre of Vienna). For BBC Television, Tim designed the costumes for the film *Alive and Kicking* and *Eastenders*. He also runs the costume department of Goldsmiths College, University of London.

Catherine Hieatt
After forming the experimental physical and visual theatre company Plastic Jungle Theatre in 1986 and touring over the course of a year Catherine Hieatt did a post graduate certificate at the Welsh College of Music and Drama, specialising in design for theatre, opera, television and film. Although based in London, she worked all over the country. In 1991 Northern Stage lured her to the North East where she worked with Neil Murray and Alan Lyddiard, culminating in her design for *Animal Farm*. Catherine was head of the scenic art department for Northern Stage for three years and a freelance

designer for other companies in the northern region. Since going freelance in 1994 she has worked with many companies including: Theatre Sans Frontieres (her design for *Notre Dame de Paris* won the Northern Electric Creative Arts Award in 1996); Northern Stage (*Animal Farm* was nominated for the Barclays and TMA Theatre Award for Best Designer in 1997); Live Theatre; The Brewery Company, Welsh National Opera, Northumberland Theatre Company, the BBC, S4C and Tyne Tees TV. Now based in the South East, her design work has included: Trestle Theatre Company's co-production with the Kherson Theatre of Ukraine on *Beggars Belief*, which has recently finished touring Britain. She plans to develop her television and film work as well as designing for new productions in physical and visual theatre. She is a member of the SBTD and Equity and she has not given up beer tasting. Salute!

Simon Higlett
Simon Higlett trained at Wimbledon School of Art and at The Slade. He has built up an extensive body of work in regional theatre, notably at the Royal Exchange Theatre, Manchester, West Yorkshire Playhouse, Crucible Theatre, Sheffield and Birmingham Repertory Theatre. His commitments in 1999 include Neil Simon's *The Prisoner of Second Avenue* (West End), *Resurrection* (Houston Grand Opera) and *Peer Gynt* (Royal Exchange, Manchester). Recent credits include: *Vertigo; Same Time Another Year; The Magistrate* (Savoy); *Talking Heads* (Comedy); *Lady Windermere's Fan* (Haymarket); *In a Little World of our Own* (Donmar); *Dangerous to Know* (national tour); *Dancing at Lughnasa* (Salisbury Playhouse); *Silhouette; Happy Valley* (Everyman, Liverpool); and *Our Betters, Beethoven's Tenth, Mansfield Park, The Miser, Dangerous Corner, Rope, Scenes from a Marriage* (latter three transferred to the West End), *A Doll's House, The Sisterhood, The Three Sisters, King Lear in New York* and *Double Take* (all Chichester Festival Theatre). Tours include: *Gaslight, Lunch Girls, Ricochet, The Lion in Winter.* Earlier London credits include: *Kean* (Old Vic); *Singer* (RSC, Barbican); *The Cabinet Minister* (Albery); *Making it Better* (Criterion); *Talking Heads* (Comedy); *Antony and Cleopatra* and *The Taming of the Shrew* (Haymarket); *Medea* (Young Vic); *The Mother Tongue* (Greenwich). From 1986-89 Simon was Head of Design at Regent's Park Open Air Theatre where his most recent production was *The Tempest*. Opera work includes: *Giulio Cesare, The Barber of Seville* and *The Rake's Progress* (Germany); *Don Giovanni, La Traviata, La Cenerentola, Cosi fan Tutte, The Marriage of Figaro, The Magic Flute, La Traviata* (Music Theatre, London); *Seraglio* (Scottish Opera); and costumes for *Der Rosenkavalier* (Marseilles Opera).

Martina Hildebrandt
Martina Hildebrandt has been working as a freelance set and costume designer since 1991, finding an affinity with small-scale venues where directors benefit from her effective and practical design style. She also production managed, built sets, props and furniture, made costumes, all from her small London workshop. Martina spent four productive years at the New End Theatre, Hampstead as Resident Designer where she enjoyed a successful collaboration with director Jon Harris. They also took their productions to other venues, including the successful tour of *Gimple the Fool* and *The Last Demon*. She also worked with visiting companies on productions

ranging from new works through to classical drama. Productions included: *Victoriana, Romeo and Juliet, A Midsummer Night's Dream, The Seven Year Itch, Macbeth, When the Barbarians Came* and *The Provoked Husband*. More recently she worked as designer at the Arts Educational Schools. Productions included: *Godspell, And the World Goes Round, Little Shop of Horrors, The Innocent Mistress, The Four Twins, The Balcony, My Sister in this House, Les Parent Terribles* and *The Dark at the Top of the Stairs*. Martina has managed to combine her life in the theatre with that of an artist and her own greeting card publications.

Guy Hoare
Guy Hoare trained with the National Youth Theatre (NYT) and at Oxford University. He worked on seven shows with the NYT in London and on tour (1992-4). In 1997 he won the Cameron Mackintosh Award, designed the lighting for Fringe First winner Life's a Gatecrash and won the Total Theatre Award for The Trial at the Edinburgh Festival. Other designs include: Sir Harrison Birtwistle's *Pulse Shadows* (Royal Festival Hall and UK tour), *No Fool Like an Old Fool* (Pegasus Theatre, Oxford and UK tour), *Faustus in the Underworld* (UK tour), *Twelfth Night* (Phoenix Hall, Osaka and Japanese tour), *Macbeth* and *Taming of the Shrew* (Tokyo Globe and Japanese tour); *Play and Ritual* (Riverside Studios), *The Country Wife, Goodnight Desdemona (Good Morning Juliet)* and *Cyrano de Bergerac* (The Bridewell), *Marisol* (Southwark Playhouse), *The Cradle Will Rock* (BAC); *Colours of Living* (Finborough) and *Kingdom on Earth* (Landor); *The Alchemist, The Oxford Greek Plays, The Playboy of the Western World, Ghetto, Dirk* and *All My Sons* (all at Oxford Playhouse) and Susannah York's production of *Look Back in Anger* (Old Fire Station). He also designed the lighting for the world premiere of *Liberty Street* (HMP Wolds, Hull for Summit Arts) and is designing their next show there in March 1999.

Dominie Hooper
Dominie Hooper studied theatre design at Nottingham Trent Polytechnic, graduating in 1992. In 1998 she received an Arts Council bursary to spend a year at the Octagon Theatre, Bolton. Here she has designed: *The Daughter in Law, Two, Pat and Margaret* and co-designed *The Mikado* with Richard Foxton; also *Hamlet* (Octagon Youth Theatre) and a collaboration with Paines Plough on its national tour of *Northern Exposure*. Freelance work prior to joining the Octagon includes: national tours of *Sea of Faces, Little White Lies* and *Birthday* (Theatre Alibi); *The Night before Christmas* (a collaboration between the RSC and Theatre Alibi); installation and site-specific work for Clanvanfrie with S.A.F.E. (Tramway and Traverse Theatre); *The Terratonia Show* (ICA, London); *Burn* (Union Chapel, Islington); *Platform 4* (Railway Arches, Exeter) and *The Pales* (Spacex Gallery, Exeter). Children's work includes: *Ssh, Telling Tales* and *Broken Angel* (Roundabout TiE); *Mirror Mirror* and *A Spell of Cold Weather* (Theatre Centre); and *Fly by Night, All at Sea, Sarawak* and *The Goose* (Theatre Alibi). Dominie is currently preparing to return to freelance work.

Pamela Howard
Professor Pamela Howard is one of Britain's leading, practising scenographers. She trained at Birmingham College of Arts and Crafts and the Slade School of Fine Art, London. Her many theatre credits

include: *Yerma, School for Wives* and *Happy Birthday Brecht* at the RNT Lyttleton Theatre in 1998; *Henry IV Parts 1 & 2* (English Touring Theatre and Old Vic, London); *The Seagull* and *Hedda Gabler*, awarded Best Touring Production (English Touring Theatre and Donmar Warehouse, London); *Othello, The Taming of the Shrew, Elgar's Rondo* and *A Patriot for Me* (Royal Shakespeare Company); *Rose Tattoo*, nominated for TMA Best Design Award (Theatr Clwyd and 1999 London revival); and productions for Birmingham Repertory Theatre, Nottingham Playhouse, Chichester Festival Theatre and Tramway, Glasgow. Pamela was founder of the European Scenography Centres and the MA Scenography Course based at Central Saint Martin's College of Art and Design in London, with centres in Utrecht, Prague, Seville, Helsinki and Zurich. She is Artistic Director of *Scenofest*, an annual international festival of scenography held in a different city each year. Other work includes: General Commissioner for Britain at Prague Quadrennial 1995 (Gold Medal for British Exhibit); Chair of British Education Commission for OISTAT (Organisation Internationale de Scénografes, Techniciens et Architectes de Théâtre); writer of many articles and books on scenography and theatre design; curator of *Ralph Koltai Retrospective*, London and International Tour; producer of *Concerto Barroco* (Opera Transatlantica, Caracas for London International Festival of Theatre 1999).

Richard Hudson
Richard Hudson was born in Zimbabwe and educated in Zimbabwe and England. He attended Wimbledon School of Art. He is the British Scenography Commissioner to OISTAT (Organisation Internationale de Scénografes, Techniciens et Architectes de Théâtre). His designs for the theatre include: *Andromache, One Way Pendulum, Too Clever by Half, Bussy d'Ambois, The Tempest* and *Candide* for the Old Vic (for which he won a Lawrence Olivier Award); *The Master Builder, Clockwork Orange, Travesties* and *The Cherry Orchard* for the Royal Shakespeare Company; *The Misanthrope, Volpone, Blue Remembered Hills* and *The Ends of the Earth* for The Royal National Theatre; *The Emperor* for The Royal Court; *Desire* and *Hippolytos* for the Almeida, and *La Bête* in New York and London. He designed the sets for *Into The Woods* in the West End and *The Lion King* in New York and Tokyo. In 1998, he won a Tony Award for his work on the *Lion King*. For opera his designs include: *The Queen of Spades, Eugene Onegin, Ermione, Manon Lescaut* and *Cosi fan Tutte* for Glyndebourne Festival Opera; *The Merry Widow* and *Die Meistersinger von Nurnberg* for the Royal Opera, Covent Garden; *Samson et Dalila* for the Metropolitan Opera, New York; *The Rake's Progress* for Chicago Lyric Opera and the Saito Kinen Festival in Japan; *Figaro's Wedding* and *The Force of Destiny* for English National Opera; *Ernani, Guillaume Tell* and *Les Contes d'Hoffmann* for the Vienna State Opera; *I Puritani* for Gran Teatro la Fenice in Venice; *L'Inganno Felice* for the Rossini Opera Festival in Pesaro; *Lucia di Lammermoor* in Zurich and at the Bayerisches Staatsoper Munich; *La Vie Parisienne, Candide, The Vanishing Bridegroom* and *Maria Stuarda* for Scottish Opera; and *A Night at the Chinese Opera* and *Count Ory* for Kent Opera.

Gabriella Ingram

Gabriella Ingram trained at Wimbledon School of Art, after which she worked as an assistant at Opera North. She has designed *The Tales of Hoffmann* (The Swan Theatre, Stratford-upon-Avon) and the set for *La Traviata* (Theatre Royal, Brighton) both for Opera Box; *Il Signor Bruschino* (Oxford Playhouse); a touring *La Traviata* (Pimlico Opera); *The Marriage of Figaro* and *Samson et Delila* (Blackheath Concert Halls). Theatre work includes: Timothy West's production of *The Soldier's Tale* (Queen Elizabeth Hall); *Don Carlos* (Lyric Theatre Studio, Hammersmith); *Wuthering Heights* (Theatre Royal, Bath); *Oedipus* and *The Haunted House* (Bridge Lane theatre); and for dance, costumes for Ra Ra Zoo (Riverside Studios); Gandini Juggling and Angika (The Place). She has also designed costumes for Madame Tussauds.

Robert Innes Hopkins

Robert Innes Hopkins' theatre designs include: *Happy End* (Nottingham Playhouse); *Miss Julie* (Young Vic); *My Mother Said I Never Should* (Oxford Stage Company); *Hunting Scenes From Lower Bavaria* and *Fatzer Materia* (Gate Theatre); *The Seagull* and *The Wasp Factory* (West Yorkshire Playhouse); and *Othello* (Washington DC). Robert won the 1996 Critics' Circle Designer of the Year Award for *The Comedy of Errors* (Royal Shakespeare Company) and *The Weavers* (Gate Theatre). In 1997 he won the Theatrical Management Association's Designer of the Year Award for *The Wasp Factory* and *My Mother Said I Never Should*. Dance designs include: *Diction* (The Place), *Swinger* (The Place/BBC2) and *Should Accidentally Fall* (BBC2) all for Yolande Snaith Theatre Dance. Opera designs include: *Eugene Onegin* (French Institute); Ghosts (Royal Opera House at Riverside Studios); Peter Grimes (Cambridge); and *The Bartered Bride* (Opera North). He was production designer on Don Boyd's film *Lucia*. Robert is also a former member of Primitive Science whose work includes *Hunger* (Purcell Room/Young Vic Studio), *Spell* and *Imperfect Librarian* (Young Vic Studio).

Mamoru Iriguchi

Mamoru Iriguchi trained in Theatre Design at the Nottingham Trent University, having worked as a set and lighting designer for one of the few regional repertory theatres in Japan, the ACM Theatre in Mito City. Design work for the ACM Theatre includes: *Noh Plays* by Yukio Mishima, *Twelfth Night* by William Shakespeare, *Yaoya-Ohichi* by Shuji Terayama and *Bacteria* by Hirohisa Hasegawa. Work as an assistant designer includes: *The Glass Menagerie* by Tennessee Williams, *Sango-Taisetsu* by Nanboku Tsuruya, *A Doll's House* by Henrik Ibsen and *Henry VI* by Luigi Pirandello. Mamoru also accompanied both domestic and international tours of the Suzuki Company of Toga led by the director, Tadashi Suzuki and worked in Toga village, where the company possessed four theatres which helped to stage international theatre festivals.

Martin Johns

Martin Johns started at the Belgrade Theatre, Coventry and was then Head of Design at Newcastle, York and Leicester. West End shows include: *Masterclass* (Old Vic and Wyndham's); *Passion Play* (Wyndham's); *West Side Story* (Her Majesty's); *The Hired Man* (Astoria); *The Entertainer* (Shaftesbury); *Let the Good Stones Roll* (Ambassadors); *Brigadoon* (Victoria Palace); *Rolls Hyphen Royce* (Shaftesbury); *A Piece of My Mind* (Apollo); *The Secret Life of Cartoons* (Aldwych); *Mack and Mabel* (Piccadilly); and the set for *The Romans in Britain* (RNT: Olivier Theatre). Martin also designed the set for *Me and My Girl* (Leicester Haymarket, Adelphi Theatre, London, Broadway, Berlin, Japan, Australia, South Africa and the British and American tours) and was nominated for a Drama Desk Award and a Tony Award in America. Other recent work includes: the 1992 *York Cycle of Medieval Mystery Plays*; the British premiers of *Marching for Faysa* (Royal Court Theatre Upstairs) and *Carrington* (Minerva Theatre, Chichester); *Carousel, Merrily We Roll Along* and *Guys and Dolls* (Leicester Haymarket); *Cabaret, Assassins* and *A Chorus Line* (Derby Playhouse); *Talking Heads 1 and 2* (Bolton Octagon); *Second from Last in the Sack Race* (Harrogate Theatre); *Love off the Shelf* (Harrogate Theatre and Nuffield Theatre, Southampton); and the 1998 century season in Keswick of *84 Charing Cross Road, Just Between Ourselves, The Late Edwina Black* and *The Golden Age of Gossip*.

Mark Jonathan

Mark Jonathan began lighting in London in 1973. He was based at Glyndebourne Opera from 1978 until 1992. Since 1993 he has been Head of Lighting at the Royal National Theatre, London. Opera lighting designs include: *Falstaff* (Los Angeles Opera); *La Finta Semplice* (Potsdam Sanssouci); *Die Entführung aus dem Serail* (Strasbourg and Caen); *Venus and Adonis* and *Dido and Aeneas* (Gent & Antwerp); *Carmen* (Tel Aviv); *Orpheus and Euridice* (Scottish Opera); *The Rake's Progress, Il Barbiere di Seviglia, Die Entführung, Idomeneo, Cosi fan Tutte* and *Albert Herring* (Glyndebourne Touring Opera); *Albert Herring* (Rome and Reggio Emiglia); *The Seraglio, Gianni Schicchi, Cavalleria Rusticana, Rigoletto, The Barber of Seville, Betly,* and *Pagliacci,* (Holland Park); *The Barber of Seville* (Opera Northern Ireland); *Orlando* (York Festival); *Cavalleria Rusticana* and *The Grace of Todd* (Opera East). Ballet designs include: *Far from the Madding Crowd, The Protecting Veil, Powder, The Prospect Before Us* (Birmingham Royal Ballet); *Landschaft und Errinerung and Exilium* (Stuttgart Ballet). He has lit over 70 plays in London and throughout the UK. At the Royal National Theatre designs include: *Skylight* (Cottesloe, Wyndham's, Vaudeville, UK tour and Bergen); *Titus Andronicus* (Cottesloe, West Yorkshire Playhouse and Almagro); *Inadmissible Evidence,* (Lyttelton Theatre). Other recent work includes: *Marlene* (Lyric Theatre, London, Paris, British and Irish tours); *Snake in the Grass* (Peter Hall Company); *Sweet Charity* (Victoria Palace).

Robert Jones

Robert Jones trained at Central School of Art and Design. This was followed by extensive repertory work at Oldham, Newcastle, Nottingham and West Yorkshire Playhouse as Head of Design. Elsewhere, theatre work includes: *Private Lives, Look Back In Anger* (Bristol Old Vic); *The Secret Rapture* (Los Angeles Drama-Logue Critic's Award); *Colours* (Abbey Theatre Dublin); *Romeo and Juliet, Rope, Dangerous Corner* and *Toad of Toad Hall* (Birmingham Rep); *Democracy* and *Crossing the Equator* (The Bush Theatre); *A Collier's Friday Night, Bold Girls, Back Up The Hearse, Lucky Sods, Morning and Evening* and *The Flight into Egypt* (Hampstead Theatre); *Getting Attention* (Royal Court); *Loot* (Theatre of Comedy); *East Lynn* (Greenwich); *The Rivals* (Derby Playhouse and Philadelphia); *Proposals* (West Yorkshire Playhouse - TMA Best Design Nomination); *When We are Married* (Chichester Festival Theatre and West End) and *Saturday, Sunday, Monday* (Chichester). Work in the West End includes: *Rosencrantz and Guildenstern are Dead, The Prime of Miss Jean Brodie, The Killing of Sister George, Black Comedy* and *The Real Inspector Hound, The Goodbye Girl, The Pope and the Witch,* and *Jolson* (also Toronto and USA tour). For the Royal Shakespeare Company: *Pentecost, Henry VIII* (also New York and Washington), *The Merchant of Venice, The Herbal Bed, Cyrano de Bergerac* (both also West End), *Romeo and Juliet, The Winter's Tale* and *Othello.* Opera includes: *The Elixir of Love* (English National Opera) and *Der Rosenkavalier* (Wuppertal and Gelsenkirchen).

Sophie Jump

Sophie Jump studied at Central Saint Martins College of Art and Design, graduating in 1992. In 1993 she designed *Full Moon* by Caradog Pritchard, directed by Helena Kaut-Howsen at Theatr Clwyd. This production was adapted for a tour of Wales and again for the Young Vic, London, finally going to the Kontakt Theatre Festival in Torun, Poland. In 1996 she designed *The Tempest* directed by Nancy Meckler, for a Shared Experience international tour. Recently she has collaborated with AandBC Theatre Company on *Twelfth Night* in the garden at Lincoln's Inn during August 1998, and on a revival of *If I Were Lifted Up from Earth* at Lincoln's Inn Chapel, in December 1998. During 1994 she became involved in the founding of a dance company - Seven Sisters Group - and has worked with choreographer Susanne Thomas several times a year since then as costume designer. Productions include: *Time of Standstill* which toured to several London venues and was part of the 1996 'Evolution' season at The Place Theatre; *Silence* at the Round Chapel, Hackney; and *Trainstations* at Kings Cross, Waterloo International, Birmingham New Street and Leeds stations. Plans for 1999 include a piece based on *Salome* to be performed at St Pancras Hotel as part of Spring Loaded.

Spyros Koskinas

Spyros Koskinas was born in Greece and studied at the Vacalo School of Art in Athens. He then went on to study Theatre Design at Croydon College of Art, Central School of Art and Design and The Slade School of Art. Most recent work includes: *Family Viewing* (Northern Media School, Sheffield); *Sacura* (Axia Co, Athens); *Sally Burgess' Women* (Lyric Theatre, Hammersmith); *The Parade* (Theatre Lab Co, Chelsea Centre Theatre); costumes for *Memory Man* (Anglia TV); *Ein Spiel mit der "Zauberflöte"* (Bochumer Symphoniker, Germany); costumes for *Last Days of a Condemned Man* (Goodfellas Productions); *My Darling Oua Oua* (Hellenic Theatre Company, Athens and Cairo); *Diary of a Madman* (also director, Dusseldorf); *The Loneliness of Cotton Meadows* (Athens). Other work includes: *Carmen* (Chelmsford Opera Group); *Faust* (Gemini Opera); *La Belle Helene* (Operabout - now Opera East); *Wanting, Running, Running* (Royal Ballet School, Sadler's Wells); *Orphée aux Enfers* (Royal Academy of Music); *Flying Lines and Accident Ballroom* (Dance Umbrella, Riverside Studios); *This is What You Get* (Dance Umbrella, The Place); *Autonomy of Containers* (Transition 86 Company); *The Last Days of Malibran* (Abbey Opera); costumes for *Street Scenes* (Palace Theatre, London Lighthouse); *Agnes of God* (Etcetera); costumes for *King* (Prince Edward Theatre); costumes for *Before the Act* (Piccadilly Theatre/20th c. Vixen Promotions); *Ironmistress* (Blood & Honey Productions); *Lost in the Stars* (New Sussex Opera); *The Fairy Queen* (Opera Integra); *Don Pasquale* (Opera Brava); *The Magic Flute* (Manilva Festival, Spain); and *Matilda* (Ion Creanga Theatre, Romania).

Anthony Lamble

Anthony studied Fine Art in Cheltenham before attending the Motley Theatre Design Course. Anthony's theatre credits include several productions at Leicester Haymarket (including *Pericles, The Winter's Tale* and *The Naked*) and the Crucible Theatre, Sheffield. He has designed for The Almeida Music Festival, The Edinburgh Festival (Traverse Theatre), and The West Yorkshire Playhouse including *Burning Everest* and more recently *Exquisite Sister* (Edinburgh International Festival 1996). Other work includes: *No Man's Land* (English Touring Theatre); *Heartbreak House, Hamlet, The Comedians* and *Whole Lotta Shakin'* (Belgrade Theatre, Coventry). Productions in London include: *Three Judgements in One* and *Time and the Room* (The Gate Theatre); *Waiting for Godot* (Lyric Hammersmith and Theatre Royal, Plymouth); *Trilby and Svengali* (Shared Experience); *Trios* and *Abundance* (Riverside Studios); *King Baby* (RSC, The Pit); *Pippin, Biloxi Blues* and *The Odd Couple* (National Youth Theatre); *Iona Rain* and *Fat Janet is Dead* (Warehouse Theatre, Croydon); *The Wolves* (Paines Plough); *Moon* (Southwark Playhouse); and *The Criminals* (Lyric Studio). Productions for The Bush Theatre include: *Looking at You (Revived) Again, The Evil Doers, Pond Life, Not Fade Away, The Mortal Ash* and *All of You Mine*. Anthony's most recent projects include: *The Secret Audience* (a short film about Napoleon), *Candida* at the RNT Studio, *Dancing at Lughnasa* at this year's Edinburgh Festival and The Arts Theatre together with a revival of *Biloxi Blues*, both for The National Youth Theatre. Anthony is a member of the teaching staff at the Motley Theatre design course.

Stefanos Lazaridis

Stefanos Lazaridis has worked extensively in Britain and abroad, notably in theatre - Chichester Festival Theatre, West End, Almeida Theatre, Royal Shakespeare Company (Stratford-upon Avon and London) and opera. Since 1970 he has designed over 25 productions for English National Opera including: *Rusalka* (also Frankfurt and Rome), *Lady Macbeth of Mtsensk* (also Amsterdam), *Hansel and Gretel* (also Venice and Amsterdam) *Macbeth, Wozzeck, The Adventures of Mr Broucek* (also Munich), *Madam Butterfly* and *The Mikado* (also Los Angeles and Houston) and *Tosca* (also Florence and Houston). He has also designed operas for The Royal Opera, Scottish Opera and Opera North as well as the 1988 arena production of *Carmen* at Earl's Court and subsequently on international tour and Sky TV; and many productions on the continent and in America. Recent work includes: large-scale productions for the lake stage at the Bregenz Festival of *Der fliegende Holländer, Nabucco* and *Fidelio* (all produced by David Pountney); *La fanciulla del West* (La Scala, Milan, Turin and Tokyo); *Pelléas et Mélisande* (Nice); *Werther* (Vancouver); *I Pagliacci* and *Cavalleria Rusticana* (Staatsoper, Berlin); *The Turn of the Screw* (La Monnaie, Brussels); *Moïse et Pharaon* (1997 Rossini Festival at the Palasport, Pesaro). He has both directed and designed: *Oedipus Rex* (Opera North); *Oedipus Rex, Bluebeard's Castle* and *Maria Stuarda* (Scottish Opera); *Orphée et Eurydice* (Australian Opera); *The End of Life* (Athens) and Duran Duran's 1993 Rock Show (North American tour). Work during 1999 includes: *Katya Kabanova* (Bayerische Staatsoper, Munich); *Lucia di Lammermoor* (Tel Aviv); *The Greek Passion* (Bregenz Festival); and *Lohengrin* (Bayreuth Festival). He has won many awards including London Evening Standard and Olivier awards for his work at English National Opera and the 1998 Opernwelt German Critics' award for Designer of the Year for *Julietta* (Opera North) and *The Turn of the Screw* (La Monnaie, Brussels). Work during 1999: *Katya Kabanova* (Bayerische Staatsoper, Munich); *Lucia di Lammermoor* (Tel Aviv); *The Greek Passion* (Bregenz Festival co-production with Royal Opera, Covent Garden); and *Lohengrin* (Bayreuth Festival).

Marie-Jeanne Lecca
Marie-Jeanne Lecca was born in Bucharest where she studied at the Beaux Arts Institute. Since 1984 she has been living in London and has worked frequently with directors David Pountney and Keith Warner. As a set and costume designer her opera credits include: *Falstaff, The Stone Guest, Pelleas and Melisande, Moses* (English National Opera); *Iolanthe* (Scottish Opera); *Carmen* (Minnesota Opera, Seattle Opera, Houston Grand Opera & Teatro Regio Torino); *The Barber of Seville* (Glimmerglass Opera, USA); *The Pirates of Penzance* (D'Oyly Carte); *La Wally* (Wexford), *La Bohème* (City of Birmingham Touring Opera); *Il Trovatore* (Dortmund). She also designed the costumes for: *The Turn of the Screw* (La Monnaie, Brussels); *Salammbo* (Opera National de Paris); *Rienzi* (Weiner Staatsoper); *Julietta* (Opera North and Opera Zuid, Maastricht); *The Nose* (De Nederlandse Opera, Amsterdam); *Cavalleria Rusticana* and *I Pagliacci* (Staatsoper Unter den Linden, Berlin); *Pacific Overtures* (English National Opera); *The Adventures of Mr Broucek* (English National Opera & Bayerische Staatsoper, Munich); and most recently *Katya Kabanova* (also in Munich). Her theatre work includes sets and costumes for *As You Like It* and *La Bête Humaine* (Nottingham Playhouse) and the costumes *The Taming of the Shrew* (Royal Shakespeare Company). For television she designed the costumes *The Big One*. Current projects are *The Greek Passion* (Bregenz Festival and the Royal Opera House) and *Der Freischutz* (English National Opera), both directed by David Pountney.

Robin Linklater
Robin Linklater trained at Wimbledon in the early 1960s. He worked in a number of repertory theatres, mostly making things, before starting to teach at Nottingham Trent University (originally Trent Polytechnic). His interest in early opera started with Terry Emery at Wimbledon and in 1978 he began working with Peter Holman (Music Director) and Jack Edwards (Stage Director) re-staging 17th and 18th century English operas, which eventually led to the forming of a touring company Opera Restor'd. He has been involved with nearly all twenty three of their productions, either as a designer or supervising students of the Theatre Design course at NTU. He designed Rossi's *Orfeo* for the Boston Early Music Festival and Drottninghom Court Theatre in 1997, co-designed Haydn's *La Cantarina* and designed Scarlatti's *La Dirindina* for Opera Restor'd in 1998. He and is currently working on the designs for Cavalli's *Hercule Amante* for BEMF in Boston and Tanglewood in June 1999 which will then tour to Utrecht, Bremen and Houston, Texas in August and September.

Keith Lodwick
Keith Lodwick trained at Central School of Speech and Drama. His design work includes: *Sweeney Todd, Les Liaisons Dangereuses, The House of Bernarda Alba, Black Comedy, Don Giovanni* (Operaworks!); *Wounds to the Face, The Ruffian on the Stairs, Maud or The Madness, The Exception and the Rule*; and costumes for *If I Were Lifted Up From Earth* (Battersea Arts Centre). Keith has also directed and designed a short film *Moments in Love*. He has designed and adapted for the stage Angela Carter's *The Bloody Chamber*. The production won a Herald Angel Award at the 1997 Edinburgh Festival and was nominated for the Total Theatre Best Design Award. He has recently designed and co-adpated Angela Carter's *The Lady of the House of Love* for the British Festival of Visual Theatre.

Claire Lyth
Claire Lyth's recent designs include: *The Man Who Thinks He's It* (The Steve Coogan Show, Lyceum, London); *The Great Gatsby* (tour); *Skylight* (Vienna); *Trouble* (M6) and *The Lily and The Rose* (Al Bustan Festival, Beirut); *Macbeth* (Residenz Theatre, Munich). Claire was Head of Design at Liverpool Playhouse and Lyceum Theatre, Edinburgh. Other regional work includes: *The Winter's Tale, Hamlet, Tosca* and *Shirley Valentine* (Liverpool Everyman); *Peter Pan* and *The Three Musketeers* (Crucible Theatre, Sheffield); *As You Like It* and *Othello* (Ludlow Festival); *The Secret Garden* and *Mixed Doubles* (Watermill Theatre, Newbury); *Young Apollo* (Leatherhead); Dario Fo's *Archangels Don't Play Pinball* (Bristol Old Vic). She has worked for the English Shakespeare Company many times, productions include: *Macbeth, Twelfth Night* and *The Fantastical Legend of Dr. Faust*. For Regents Park: *All's Well That Ends Well* and *Comedy of Errors*. Other productions in London include: *The Fall* (Chelsea Centre); *Same Time Next Year* (Old Vic); *Candida* (The Arts) and *Split Second* (Lyric Hammersmith). Opera designs include: *Rigoletto* (tour for Welsh National Opera); *Cosi fan Tutte* and *The Secret Marriage* (Hong Kong); National Opera Studio Showcase '93 (Queen Elizabeth Hall); *Rags* (Spitalfields Market Opera); and *Nightingale* (Buxton Opera House). Musicals include: *Fungus the Bogeyman* (Belgrade Theatre, Coventry); *Mad and her Dad* and *Split Second* (Lyric Theatre, Hammersmith); *Oklahoma!* (national tour). She has also worked in Denmark, Germany and Vienna on many occasions.

Ian MacNeil
Ian MacNeil studied at Croydon School of Art. Opera credits include: *Medea* (Opera North); *Tristan and Isolde* (English National Opera - Olivier Award for Best Opera 1997); *Ariodante* (ENO and Welsh National Opera); and *La Traviata*, directed by Jonathan Miller (Bastille Opera, Paris). London and national tours include: *Pioneers in Ingolstadt, Don Gill of the Green Breeches* and *Jerker* (Gate Theatre, Notting Hill); *The Picture of Dorian Grey* (Lyric Theatre, Hammersmith); *Death and the Maiden, The Editing Process, This is a Chair* and *Via Dolorosa* (Royal Court). He has designed the last two DV8 shows *Enter Achilles* and *Bound to Please*. For the Royal National Theatre he designed *Machinal* which won the Critic's Circle Award and *An Inspector Calls* which won the Critic's Circle Award and an Olivier Award for Design in 1993 and is still running at the Garrick Theatre in the West End. It played on Broadway at the Royal Theater (Outer Circle Critic's Award, Drama Desk Award and a nomination for a Tony for Best Design) and there have been numerous productions around the world. Ian has recently designed a short film for Working Title, *Eight*, which was directed by Stephen Daldry and is about to start collaborating with The Pet Shop Boys on artwork and videos tied into their forthcoming album. He is currently designing *Der Freischutz* for ENO's 1999-2000 season and is adapting his designs for *Via Dolorosa* which opens in New York in March 1999.

Christine Marfleet
Christine Marfleet studied Drama at Bristol University and designed productions for the Glynne Wickham Studio. Starting out as a design assistant at Newcastle Playhouse, she gained experience with designers, directors and production teams, enabling her to develop a career as resident and freelance designer. After fifteen years designing sets and costumes for a wide range of spaces and places, extensive experience of devised and new work, theatre in education and lots of touring, she now combines teaching at Birmingham Institute of art and Design with freelance projects - focusing more often on participating as designer/devisor and making pieces for unusual and challenging locations. Exhibitions have included: *Make Space!* and the 1995 Prague Quadrennial (British entry). Work for theatre companies has included: Duke's Playhouse, Lancaster; Mercury Theatre, Colchester; Everyman Theatre, Liverpool; Tricycle Theatre, Kilburn; M6 Theatre Company; and Theatr Powys. Teaching and workshops: Wimbledon School of Art; *Make Space!* education programme; Hope Street Project.

Tanya McCallin
Tanya McCallin trained at The Central School of Art and Design. After a period designing for several principal repertory companies throughout Britain and many fringe theatres in London, she began a series of productions for Hampstead Theatre, designing: *Sparrowfall, Dusa, Fish, Stas and Vi* (also Mayfair Theatre and Paris), Mike Leigh's *Abigail's Party, Dodies* (also Ambassadors), *The Elephant Man* (also National Theatre), *The Hard Shoulder* (also Aldwych); *Sufficient Carbohydrate* by Dennis Potter (also Albery), *The Perfectionist* and Anthony Minghella's *A Little Like Drowning*. Other credits include: *Macbeth, Uncle Vanya, Betrayal* and *Mourning Becomes Electra* (Melbourne Theatre Company); *Bread, They are Dying Out, Don Juan Returns from the War* and *Who's Afraid of Virginia Woolf?* (National Theatre); *A Nightingale Sang, Before the Party* (and Apollo); *Women Beware Women* (Oxford Playhouse Company); *Ghosts* (Actors Company); *School for Scandal, The Changeling, The Homecoming, I am Who I am* and *The Late Christopher Bean* (Cambridge Theatre Company); *Travelling North* (Lyric Hammersmith); *My Mother Said I Never Should* by Charlotte Keatley (Royal Court); *Uncle Vanya*, translated by Michael Frayn (Vaudeville); *Exchange* (Nuffield and Vaudeville); *The Winter Wife* by Claire Tomalin (Nuffield and Lyric Hammersmith - nominated for the TMA Awards in 1991); Arthur Miller's *Ride Down Mount Morgan* (Wyndhams Theatre); *Obsession* and *Strictly Entre Nous* (BAC); *Hamlet* and *Richard III* (Regents Park Theatre). Tanya has designed the costumes for *Arthur Miller's After the Fall* (National Theatre); Michael Frayn's *Make and Break* (Kennedy Centre); *Streaming* (Piccadilly); and *The Perfect Ganesh* by Terrence McNally (West Yorkshire Playhouse). Opera work includes: Jonathan Miller's current *Barber of Seville* (ENO); David McVicar's *Manon* (ENO) and the costumes for his recent production of *Der Rosenkavalier* for Scottish Opera. Future plans include a production of *Albert Herring*. She is currently external examiner in Theatre Design at Central St Martins College of Art and Design.

Gary McCann
Gary McCann trained at Nottingham Trent University. Recent design work in Northern Ireland includes: *Alice's Adventures in Wonderland, The Visit, Tearing the Loom* by Gary Mitchell and *Iphigenia in Aulis* (Lyric Theatre, Belfast); *Hansel and Gretel* (Kabosh at the Riverside Theatre, Coleraine). His work in mainland Britain includes designs for: *The Tempest* (Gardner Arts Centre, Brighton); *Capital Nights* (Warehouse Theatre, Croydon); *The Swell* and *The Night before Christmas* (Devon's Theatre Alibi); and *The Quay Thing*, a season of ten site-specific performances on Exeter Quay.

Peter McKintosh
Peter McKintosh's work for theatre includes: *Burned Alive, The Black Dahlia, Demons and Dybbuks* and *The Cherry Orchard* (Method and Madness); *Killing Rasputin* (Bridewell Theatre); *Snoopy* (Watermill Theatre, Newbury); *Honk!* (Stephen Joseph Theatre, Scarborough); *Travels with my Aunt* (UK tour and Vienna); *On Borrowed Time* (Southwark Playhouse); *Pal Joey* (Theatre Royal, York); and *Noises Off* (Old Vic, Bristol). Opera: *L'Enfant et les Sortilèges* (Birmingham Conservatoire); *Die Fledermaus* and *La Bohème* (Amsterdam and UK tour); *L'Elisir d'Amore* and *The Marriage of Figaro* (Mid-Wales Opera); *Betley* with *I Pagliacci* and *The Barber of Seville* (Holland Park Opera Festival). Ballet: *Cut to the Chase* (English National Ballet). Peter is Associate Designer for Method and Madness Theatre Company.

Jocelyn Meall
Jocelyn Meall was born in Liverpool. She graduated with a degree in Theatre Design in Trent/Nottingham in 1990. From there she designed TIE shows for Roundabout, Nottingham Playhouse, Contact Theatre and Pitprop. For Liverpool Playhouse she has designed a season of new local writing in the studio and *Bouncers and Shakers* for the main auditorium. She has worked a lot with the TIPP Centre at Manchester University developing forum based workshops. In 1996-7 Jocelyn was awarded an Arts Council of England design bursary based at the Bolton Octagon. There she has designed: *Talent, Top Girls, Candida* and *Christmas Carol* in the main auditorium and *Kiss of the Spiderwoman, My Children! My Africa* and *Ghost from a Perfect Place* in the Bill Naughton Theatre.

Fred Meller
Fred Meller trained as a post graduate at The Welsh College of Music and Drama and studied Theatre at The University of Ulster, Northern Ireland. After a spell working in various capacities in a number of theatres, while also designing on the London Fringe, Fred was awarded an Arts Council Bursary and spent a year associated with The Wolsey Theatre in Ipswich. Work there included: *The Rise and Fall of Little Voice, A Chorus of Disapproval, Happy Families*, the

regional premiere of *The Thickness of Skin* and more recently *The Norman Conquests*. Other recent set and costume designs include: commissions for the homeless people's theatre company Cardboard Citizens; *Othello* (Theatre Royal, Bury St Edmunds); *Loot* (Theatre Royal, Plymouth); *A Taste of Honey* and *Telling Tales* (Nuffield Theatre, Southampton); the national tour of *Woof!* (Birmingham Stage Company); and *Talking Heads* and *Skylight* (The Watermill Theatre). With Eastern Angles Theatre Company: *The Wuffings* (a site-specific project based on the Anglo Saxon ship burial at Sutton Hoo); *David Copperfield, Fields* and *A Warning to the Curious* (from the ghost stories by M R James). Fred enjoys the challenge of all scales of touring, new writing and projects where collaboration is the vital force; building successful and lasting working relationships with directors and lighting designers.

Lucinda Meredith
For the past four years Lucinda Meredith has been studying for both a Masters Degree in Advanced Theatre Practice and Post Graduate Diploma in Theatre Design Costume at Central School of Speech and Drama. Her specialist area of inquiry being the use of design in devised and collaborative theatre practice. An equal balance of research and design work has enabled her to develop a working strategy and theory exploring how to implement collaborative design techniques through the use of game play and explorative improvisation exercises. Her research period culminated in the thesis 'The Character of Costume' and it is this that has underpinned the methodology in creating the design for *Prologue*. Prior to this research period Lucinda's theatre experience was gained by working in a technical capacity with a wide range of companies including fringe theatre, dance, opera and circus. Other academic achievements include BA (Hons) Degree in Theatre Design at Birmingham Polytechnic. Recent credits include: *Prologue* (Theatre Cryptic with The Shamans, 1998 Belfast Festival), 1998 Theatre Design Summer School (The Tron Theatre), *Fire Festival* (Expo'98, Lisbon), *Nabucco* (Glasgow Grand Opera at The Royal Scottish Academy of Music and Drama) *The Journey West* (Tripitaka Theatre Company) *Milk and Blood* (British Festival of Visual and Devised Theatre at the Battersea Arts Centre). I am currently looking to continue and develop this collaborative approach to design through design practice, further research and teaching opportunities.

Madeleine Millar
Madeleine Millar studied Theatre Design at Trent Polytechnic, Nottingham and has an MA in Art and Design from Leeds Metropolitan University. She has been working for over twenty years in children's theatre, theatre in education, community and repertory theatre. Productions include: *Gaslight, Macbeth, Hedda Gabler, Confusions* and *Mother Goose* (as a season at St. Andrews); *Simple Simon* (Stephen Joseph Theatre-in-the-Round); *Don't She Look Silly* (York Y.P.T.); *Pentabus; Mutiny on the Bounty, Face at the Window, No Smoke without Walter* (Soapbox Children's Theatre); *Flags and Bandages, Strathnever*, and *Seizing the Time* (Leeds Playhouse TiE); *Graven Images, Mountains on the Moon, Bloodlines* and *Sweet Banana Fruit Mix* (Pit Prop); *Sacred Ground* (Watford Palace TiE); *The Best* (Red Ladder); *Aladdin, The Night Garden, Glory* and *The Picture Writer* (Theatr Powys); *The Good Soldier* and *The Marvellous Boy* (Public Parts); *The Wrench* (Big Brum TiE); *Monsters of Creation* (Collar and TiE); *Fairground Attractions* and *Sea Changes* (Interplay); *The Boatbuilder - a Tapestry of Tales* (Whiteswood and Fleming Theatre and Music); *Edible City* and *Tidelines* (West Yorkshire Playhouse Theatre in Schools); *One Big Blow* (Compact). As well as designing for the theatre, Madeleine won a commission from Bauman Lyons Architects for a security screen for the Chinese Community Centre in Leeds and has exhibited her sculpture in Kendal, Halifax and Leeds. She is a part time lecturer in Performance Design at Park Lane College, Leeds.

Martin Morley
Born in 1944 Martin Morley trained at The Wimbledon School of Art: 1963-1966. Before settling in Wales in 1973, he worked at the Royal Lyceum Theatre, Edinburgh and from 1969-1972 was Head of Design at The Liverpool Playhouse. From 1973-1984 he was designer with Theatr Cymru - at the time, until it's demise in 1984, the premier Welsh Language Theatre Company. Since 1984 he has been freelance, working increasingly as a set designer for S4C, but he has continued to design one or two productions per year chiefly for Theatr Gwynedd. The nature of the population spread in Wales dictates that 90% of productions must tour around Wales's ill matched performance venues, and therein lies most of the design challenges: after deciding on the production concept, how to make each set seem at home in each different venue.

Muir
Muir has extensive experience in physical theatre; amongst other companies: Ra Ra Zoo, Scarabeus, Heir of Insanity, Momentary Fusion and Ghandini Juggling Project. Other work includes projects with Phoenix Dance Company, English National Opera Baylis Programme, Glyndebourne Opera, Glastonbury Festival and Guildhall School of Music and Drama.

Ruari Murchison
Ruari Murchison as worked in major regional theatres including Nottingham Playhouse, Crucible Theatre Sheffield, West Yorkshire Playhouse and Birmingham Rep. London work includes productions at The Young Vic, Hampstead Theatre Club, Greenwich, The Royal Court and The Royal National Theatre. Recent design work includes: *The Red Balloon* (Royal National Theatre); *The Snowman* (Sadlers Wells at the Peacock Theatre); *The Tempest, Macbeth, The Merchant of Venice, Hamlet, Frozen*, and *The Four Alice Bakers* (Birmingham Rep). Opera work includes: *Peter Grimes, Cosi fan Tutte* (Luzerner Oper); *La Cenerentola, Il Barbiere di Siviglia* (Garsington); *L'Italiana in Algeri* (Buxton); *Les Pelerins de la Mecque, ZaZa* (Wexford); *The Magic Flute* and *A Midsummer Night's Dream* (Covent Garden Festival). Ballet work includes: *The Protecting Veil* (Birmingham Royal Ballet); *Le Festin de l'Araignee* (Royal Ballet School - Royal Opera House Gala); and *Landschaft und Erinnerung* (Stuttgart Ballet); all choreographed by David Bintley. He is currently designing *West Side Story* for the Stratford Festival, Ontario.

Neil Murray
Neil Murray has been a Director at Northern Stage for seven years where he has designed all the work of the Artistic Director, Alan Lyddiard, including: *A Nightingale Sang, Entertaining Mr. Sloane, Andorra, Foreign Lands, A Clockwork Orange, Blood Wedding, A Version of Twelfth Night* and the opera *Cullercoats Tommy*. At the same time Neil has directed and designed his own productions of *Carmen, Thèrèse Raquin, She Stoops to Conquer, The Swan, They Shoot Horses Don't They?, The Long Line, Octopus Hotel* and *The Threepenny Opera* as well as directing and designing all the Northern Stage Christmas pieces: *Beauty and the Beast, The Snow Queen, Cinderella, The Sleeping Beauty, Merlin The Magnificent* and *The Princess and the Goblin*. Formerly, he was Associate Director at Dundee Rep for eleven years where he directed and designed many pieces including: *Sweeney Todd, Phantom of the Opera, 'Tis Pity She's a Whore, Equus* and *The Philanthropist*. Whilst in Scotland he designed *Kora and Klimov* (Traverse Theatre), *Dirty Linen* (Royal Lyceum Theatre), *The Tempest* (TAG Theatre Co.), and the site-specific pieces *Witches Blood I and II* with Alan Lyddiard in Dundee and City and *Amadeus* for Glasgow European City of Culture.

Dody Nash
Dody Nash studied Fine Art at Central Saint Martins College of Art and Design and History of Art and English at the University of York before training in Theatre Design at Motley. She has also worked extensively as a freelance assistant designer, model-maker and scenic painter. Much of this work has been for English National Opera. Recently designs include costumes for *Hansel and Gretel* (Baylis Programme, English National Opera) and sets for *Little Shop of Horrors* (Northcott Theatre, Exeter). Costumes designs also include: *Lucky Stiff* (Bridewell Theatre); *Tales My Lover Told Me* (Kings Head Theatre); and *With Complete Kander* (Westminster Theatre). Set and costumes designs include: *Teenage Vitriol* (Finborough Theatre); *Golem* (Bridewell Theatre); *The Libertine* (RADA); *A Small World* (Southwark Playhouse); a Samuel Beckett premiere, *First Love* (Etcetera Theatre) and *Miss Julie* (Lyric Studio Hammersmith).

Pippa Nissen
Pippa Nissen studied for her degree and diploma in architecture at Cambridge University writing her dissertation on theatrical space within the city. She also has an MA in Theatre Design from the Slade, which she passed with distinction, where her thesis was on space within Greek theatre. Part of her research included travelling to Thessaloniki and studying a production of *Ion* with the Actors' Touring Company. Designs include; *Mignon* (University College Opera); *Eugene Onegin* (Clonter Opera and Buxton Festival); *Faust* (Actors' Touring Company); *Ozolumbu Dance* (Bloomsbury Theatre); *Ken and Barb* (Guilded Balloon); *Frank and Martha Were Brothers* (Camden Studio Theatre); *The Spanish Lady* (Cambridge University Opera); *Lovebites* (Riverside Studios); and co-designed: *The Belle Vue* (ATC); and *One Flew Over the Cuckoo's Nest* (A.D.C. Cambridge). Directing and design credits include: *Dee* and *Camera Oscura* (Garage Theatre Workshop). Assistant work includes *Footfalls* with *Hildegard Bechtler* and *Lulu* with Stewart Laing. Pippa divides her time between architecture and theatre design, with a special interest in the design of theatre buildings and the link between the two disciplines having taught theatre design workshops for architects at the Architectural Association and Cambridge University. She is represented by the Designers Formation agency.

Christopher Oram
Christopher Oram trained at Northbrook College, Worthing. Designs include: *Good* (Donmar Warehouse); *Twelfth Night* and *What the Butler Saw* (Crucible Theatre, Sheffield); *The 6th Stonewall Equality Show* (Royal Albert Hall); *The Doctor's Dilemma* (Almeida Theatre and tour); *The Bullet* (Donmar Warehouse); *All My Sons* (Bristol Old Vic); *Just One World* (Aachen, Germany); *The Deep Blue Sea, As You Like It* and *The Last Yankee* (Mercury Theatre, Colchester); *Old Wicked Songs* (Bristol Old Vic & Gielgud Theatre); *Giovanni's Room* (Drill Hall); *A Week with Tony* (Finborough); *All Tomorrow's Parties* (Old Red Lion and Royal Exchange); *Seeing Marie* (Old Red Lion).

Kate Owen
Kate Owen trained at the Central School of Art and Design with Ralph Koltai. She has designed over 150 first productions of new plays, new dance and circus. She teaches theatre design at King Alfred's University College, and other design schools. Recent work includes: *King Arthur and the Knights of the Occasional Table* (Lip Service); a 'non-linear multi-media' version of *A Midsummer Night's Dream* (The Anvil, Basingstoke); *Alice* (Nottingham Playhouse); *Get a Life* and *Dick and his Dog* (Cardboard Citizens); *Landslide* (West Yorkshire Playhouse); *Move Over Moriarty* (Lip Service); *The Hand* (Gay Sweatshop Theatre Company); *Loot* and *Entertaining Mr Sloane* (Birmingham Repertory Theatre); *The Madness of Esme* and *Shaz* (Royal Court); *Stairway to Heaven* (Shared Experience at St Anne's Churchyard, Soho); *Familiar Feelings* and *The Visitor*, which she co-wrote and directed (Theatre Centre at Riverside Studios and on national tour); and *Betrayal* (Graham Cowley Productions at the Thorndike Theatre, Leatherhead, the Battersea Arts Centre and on national tour). She was the site designer for the Royal National Theatre production of *Oh What a Lovely War!*, recently on tour in England and Wales.

Celia Perkins
Celia Perkins trained in Theatre Design at Croydon College and the Slade School of Fine Art. On leaving, she designed small-scale Theatre in Education and fringe productions including *Adam Bede* at The Orange Tree, shows for the Edinburgh Fringe, Theatre Venture and the National Youth Dance Company. Celia has worked at the Oldham Coliseum Theatre for the past five years, initially as a scenic artist, then Assistant Designer and for the past three years as Resident Designer. The Coliseum is a repertory theatre whose fortunes have changed drastically over this time, coming perilously close to closure and forced to re-evaluate its role in the community. It has been rewarded for this by becoming an extremely popular and loyally attended theatre. Designing for the Coliseum is never dull and can range from ultra naturalism to extravagant and spectacular pantomimes, intimate one handers or from musicals to studio productions. Her designs for the Coliseum include such diverse productions as the annual pantomime: *Dick Whittington, Aladdin* and *Cinderella* (nominated for the Manchester Evening News Best Design Team Award); *to Me Mam Sez, Y' shunta' Joined* and *A Different Way Home* (all nominated for the Manchester Evening News Best Design Team Award).

Tom Phillips RA
Tom Phillips, designer and translator, was born in London where he still lives and works. As an internationally established artist and prominent Royal Academician he is represented in museum collections worldwide. He is best known for his book *A Humument* and his work on *Dante's Inferno* which he translated and illustrated (as co-director of the TV version he won the Italia Prize). Major retrospectives of his paintings have been held on both sides of the Atlantic including National Portrait Gallery, Yale Center, Royal Academy, Musée d'Art Moderne, Paris and in 1997 Dulwich Picture Gallery. His musical compositions include the opera *Irma* which has been recorded several times and the song suite *Six of Hearts* performed in this year's Darmstadt Festival. His most recent theatre project, also in association with David Freeman, was designing *The Winter's Tale* for the opening of the Shakespeare's Globe Theatre in London.

Dana Pinto
Dana Pinto is an up and coming designer who trained at Wimbledon School of Art, graduating with a degree in Theatre Design. She has designed various student productions as well as contemporary plays for the fringe including: *Quilt - a Musical Celebration*. Amongst her theatre designs she has worked as a model animator and has also constructed sets for Broadway Theatre, London and Shepperton Film Studios. Further work includes: *Oraculos*, directed by Enrique Vargas and *Taller de Investigación de la Imagen Dramatica*, Ayuntamiento de Mostoles as part of the London International Festival of Theatre 1997.

Tom Piper
Tom Piper graduated from Trinity College, Cambridge before training at the Slade School of Art. Designs include: *The Birthday, Blinded By The Sun* and *Oh What a Lovely War!* (Royal National Theatre); *The Broken Heart, Spring Awakening, A Patriot for Me, Much Ado About Nothing, The Spanish Tragedy, Bartholomew Fair, Measure for Measure, Troilus and Cressida* and *A Month in the Country* (Royal Shakespeare Company); *The Crucible* and *Six Characters in Search of an Author* (Abbey Theatre, Dublin); *The Master Builder* (Royal Lyceum Theatre, Edinburgh); *Waking, Tulip Futures, Ripped, Kindertransport, The Rock Station* and *My Goat* (Soho Theatre Company - London Fringe Design Award 1992/93 for Rock Station); *Endgame, Dumbstruck, Macbeth, Cinderella* and *Jack and the Beanstalk* (Tron Theatre, Glasgow); *The Price* (York Theatre Royal); *The Way of the World* (Lyric, Hammersmith), *The Masked Ball* (Dublin Grand Opera); *The Duchess of Malfi* (Greenwich and Wyndham's); *The Philanderer* and *Sweet Panic* (Hampstead); *The Cherry Orchard* (Nottingham Playhouse); *Golem* (Northern Stage Company with Northern Sinfonia); *The Dark River, Cat with Green Violin, His Majesty, We the Undersigned, Mrs Warren's Profession* (Orange Tree, Richmond); *No-one Writes to the Colonel* (Lyric Hammersmith Studio); *Storming, Backpay, Cockroach* and *Who?* (Royal Court Theatre Upstairs); *Kindertransport* (Watford Palace and Vaudeville); *A Cat in the Ghetto* (Tabard Theatre, Chiswick - Charrington London Fringe Award for Best Design 1989/90); *Noyes Fludde* (St James's Church, Piccadilly and Royal Albert Hall); *Wallace and Gromit* (national tour); *Scissor Happy* (Duchess); and *Dealer's Choice* (Theater inder Josephstadt, Vienna).

Jason Redgrave
Jason Redgrave trained at Nottingham Trent University, graduating in 1993. Most recently he has been the resident designer for Salamander Theatre Company, a TiE company, on a wide variety of shows including: *Kick*, a drug awareness project; *Vackies*, a history project about life in the Second World War; *The Blue Marble*, a devised interactive game show raising awareness of the environment; and *Red Riding Hood*, both as a touring Christmas show and in the Chiswick Town Hall Theatre. Other productions include: set and costume design for *Silly Cow* by Ben Elton (Andrews Lane Theatre, Dublin and The Grace Theatre at the Latchmere Pub, London); costume design for *Michelangelo's Slave* by Atar Hadari (Wimbledon Studio Theatre); set design for *The Diary of Anne Frank* by Francis Goodrich and Albert Brackett (Pavilion Theatre, Brighton); assistant designer for *Miss Roach's War* adapted by Richard Kane (Wimbledon Studio Theatre and Croydon Warehouse Theatre) and *The Rape of Lucretia* by Benjamin Britten (Battersea Arts Centre).

Christopher Richardson
Christopher Richardson studied Interior Design at the Royal College of Art under Sir Hugh Casson. He won a silver medal for experimental theatre design and was part of the winning Prix d'Etranger team at the *Paris Biennale* of 1965 and prizewinner with the same team the following year at the Liberec Symposium in Czechoslovakia.
He taught design, English and then Drama for twenty years setting up the Uppingham Theatre. In 1985/6 he started Theatre Futures, with John Faulkner, and The Pleasance Theatre Festival for the Edinburgh Festival Fringe. In 1995 he raised money for and organised the conversion, on the border of Camden and Islington, of the London General Omnibus Company's 19th-century wood store into a 280 seat theatre Pleasance London. He has been heavily involved in the design of theatres from Keswick and Edinburgh to Brighton and St Helier. He has designed settings to support, amongst others, Mel Smith, Clive Anderson, Nick Hancock, Richard Curtis, Angus Deayton, Philip Pope, Rowan Atkinson, Howard Goodall, Max Wall, Mollie Sugden, The National youth Music Theatre and productions for Pleasance London and Edinburgh. And he has paid for a few drinks on the way. He is currently Chairman of the Society of British Theatre Designers.

Isabel Robson
Isabel Robson graduated in theatre design from Central Saint Martins College of Art and Design in 1997. During her studies she received a Kirk EC travel grant to research contemporary French scenography. This lead her to take part in Jacque Lecoq's experimental scenography workshop in Paris. Following a UNESCO-Aschberg stage design residency in Tashkent, Uzbekistan, Isabel designed Oedipus Dance Company's *Lambeth Orpheus* (Brix Theatre) and *Sleeper* (4D Company at The Place and on tour). In 1998 she assisted on *The Tempest* and *Faustus 53* (Berliner Ensemble, Germany). This experience fed into her subsequent designs for Intoto Productions' new play for Brecht's 100th Anniversary (Riverside Studios and tour).

Marise Rose
See entry for Ali Allen and Marise Rose

Cathy Ryan
Cathy Ryan studied Fine Art at Bristol Polytechnic, and post-graduate Theatre Design at the Bristol Old Vic Theatre School. Design work has included: *Strange Fruit, City Echoes, Take My Husband*, and *It's a Bobby's Job* (Liverpool Playhouse); *The Conduct of Life, Struggle of the Black Man and the Dogs, Vera Baxter, The Struggle* (Gate Theatre, Notting Hill); *Streetwalkers* (Bush Theatre, London); *Weissman and Copperface* (Traverse Theatre, Edinburgh); *Loot* (Swan Theatre, Worcester); *Heimerbeit* (Battersea Arts Centre Young Directors Award); *Fen* and *Masterpieces* (Theatre Royal, Stratford East); *Pretend We're Friends* (Quicksilver Theatre for Children); *Of Mice and Men, In Bed with Billy Cotton, Relatively Speaking, Romeo and Juliet, Good Golly Miss Molly, The Good Companions, It's a Lovely Day Tomorrow* and *Twelfth Night* (Belgrade Theatre, Coventry); *Too Much too Young* (London Bubble and tour); *Romeo and Juliet* and *The Good Companions* (New Victoria, Stoke); *The Cunning Little Vixen* (The Baylis Programme of Opera Workshops ENO); *The Marriage of Figaro* (Pimlico Opera); *Thark, When the Wind Blows, Dangerous Corner* and *David Copperfield* (New Victoria, Stoke); *Way Past Cool* (Royal Court Young People's Theatre); *Flat 4D, The Gap, Stop the Rot* and *What a Life* (Cardboard Citizens and Deaf Theatre Forum at the London Bubble). Film and TV work includes: *Rif Raf, Ladybird Ladybird, Young Soul Rebels, Institute Benjamenta* and *Brookside*.

Alan Schofield
Alan Schofield has designed scenery since childhood, starting with toy theatres and then converting hen houses and any other space he could find into improvised theatres. Despite this early start and a lifetime devoted to amateur theatre, Alan became a professional designer late in life, having been a documentary film maker for over 20 years. From 1989 to 1996 he was resident designer and art teacher at Elmhurst Ballet School. Since working freelance he has maintained his contact with young people through Show Shack Musical Theatre School and The Surrey County Youth Theatre which staged the British premier of the American musical, Archy and Mohitabel in 1997. He also taught Theatre Production Techniques at Brooklands College. Recent productions include: *Aladdin, Noddy, Puss in Boots, A Dragon for Dinner, The Winter Thing, Mr. Fox* and *The Wizard of Oz* (Novello Theatre); *Stepping Out, Cinderella, The Boy Friend, Humpty Dumpty, Old Time Music Hall* and *Sleeping Beauty* (Prince Regent Intimate Theatre). Other credits include *Me and My Girl* and *Singing in the Rain* (StageSets of London) and various themed events for Best Events of Maidenhead. Alan Schofield recently came full circle making the Novello auditorium look like a toy theatre.

Nettie Scriven
Nettie Scriven has worked extensively since 1980 in a variety of spaces including schools, community centres, art centres, art galleries, studio theatres and main stages with particular interest in new writing, devising performance installations, dance, multi-media and site-specific work. Productions include: *A Little Princess* (Yvonne Arnaud Theatre); *Stepper Joe* and *The Waltz* (West Yorkshire Playhouse); *Crivelli's Garden* (Theatre Centre); *Rooms* (Glasshouses Dance Company); *One for Sorrow* (Hi-jinx Theatre Company); *The Snow Spider* (Sherman Theatre, Cardiff); *The Lost Child* and *Plague of Innocence* (1988 Best Young People's Theatre production - Crucible Theatre, Sheffield); *Hamlet* (Contact Theatre); and *The Scam* (Traverse Theatre). Nettie has a combined honours degree in Drama and Sociology from Birmingham University and an M A in Fine Art. She is a senior lecturer in Theatre Design at The Nottingham Trent University and lives in Nottingham with her two young children.

Jan P Sendor
Jan P Sendor worked in repertory theatre then university. Stratford East and The Fun Palace with Joan Littlewood followed by a long and varied career as a lighting designer, technician, set designer, performer, director, fire-eater, technical director and facilitator. Almost all of this has been in the subsidised theatre, arts centres, derelict factories and dance halls with excursions into the West End, outdoor events and latterly teaching.

Juliet Shillingford
Juliet trained at Ravensbourne and Croydon Colleges of Art, receiving a degree in Fine Art and a diploma in Theatre Design. She was awarded an Arts Council training bursary later becoming Associate Designer for the Redgrave Theatre, Farnham and the Library Theatre, Manchester. Freelance work includes productions for: Lyric Theatre, Hammersmith; King's Head, Islington; Oldham Coliseum; Perth Theatre; and Leicester Haymarket Studio. Recent work includes: *Peter Pan, Mail Order Bride, Brothers of the Brush, Waiting for Godot, The Seduction of Anne Boleyn* and *Alice in Wonderland* (Nuffield Theatre, Southampton); and *Piaf* and *Richard III* (Haymarket Theatre, Leicester).

Georgina Shorter
Georgina Shorter studied Fashion Design and Production at La Salle International Fashion School in Singapore (1991-1993). On moving to England, she studied Theatre Design at Central Saint Martins College of Art and Design, graduating in 1996 with a BA (Hons) Degree. Georgina made her debut in 1997 as a set designer with the Trinity Theatre Company (Tunbridge Wells, Kent), for Peter Nichols' *Passion Play*, director Francesca Gilpin; lighting designer. Bruce J. Williams. Later the same year she designed the set and costumes for The Trinity Theatre Company's Christmas box-office hit production of C S Lewis' *The Lion, the Witch and the Wardrobe*; this production was in collaboration with Terry Murphy Scenery Ltd.
Since then she has worked as Art Director and Production Designer for several short films including: *Lost in Space* (script and direction by David Raedeker); *The Lullaby*, filmed at Pinewood Studios (script and direction by Andrew Hannan); *Hotline* (script and direction by Tharsin Guner); and *Closing Hours*, Which has gone on to win numerous awards at New York short film festivals in 1998 (script and direction by Michael Lim). She has also worked as a freelance costumier for The Olympic Dance Company, the current West End show *Beauty and the Beast*, and George Lucas' forthcoming *Star Wars* film which opens in the spring of 1999.

Ian Sommerville
Ian Sommerville is a set and lighting designer for opera, theatre, dance and architectural projects. He is also an interior designer, a painter and a fine artist. He is currently lighting consultant to the National Opera Studio. Recent work as a designer includes *Andrea Chénier* (Norwegian National Opera); and as a lighting designer: *Un Ballo in Maschera* (Opéra de Monte Carlo); *The Aspern Papers* (Guildhall School of

Music and Drama); *Mr Puntilla and his man Matti* (Almeida Theatre); *Toupees and Snaredrums* (Abbey Theatre, Dublin). His recent exhibition of art at The Concorde Gallery in London was based on his designs for *Poisoned Silence* (Opera North Community Project) which was also entered as part of the British exhibit at the 1995 Prague Quadrennial. Current projects include lighting for *Les Miserables* (Goteborg Opera) and church lighting for the Millennium.

George Souglides
George Souglides studied at Middlesex and Kingston Universities and at Motley Theatre Design course. Recent opera work includes: *A Midsummer Night's Dream* (Aldeburgh Festival/Britten Pears Opera); *L'elisir D'amore* (Greek National Opera); *Cosi Fan Tutte* (Scottish Opera Go Round); *The Rape of Lucretia* (Britten Pears Opera, Snape Maltings); *The Reluctant Highwayman* (Broomhill Opera); *La Traviata, Cosi fan Tutte, Don Pasquale, Gianni Schicchi* and *I Pagliacci* and *L'elisir D'amore* (Castleward Opera); *The Tales of Hoffmann* (Pavilion Opera); *Maria Stuarda* (Opera Northern Ireland tour); in theatre: *The White Bird Passes* (Dundee Repertory Theatre); *Nana* (Lyric Theatre Hammersmith); Filumena *Marturano* (Drama Centre, London); *Merlin* (Arts Threshold, London); *Man, Beast and Virtue* (National Theatre of Cyprus); *Measure for Measure* (Royal Lyceum Theatre); *The Lady Aoi and Hanjo* (Gate Theatre, London); *Broken Nails* (St. Peter's Cathedral, Belfast); *Comrades* (Drama Centre); *Breaking the Frame* (Etcetera Theatre); in dance: associate designer for *Fearful Symmetries* (Royal Ballet, Royal Opera House); *Alistair Fish* (BBC 2 Dance for Camera); *The Scattering Matrix* (ICA Dance Umbrella). He has assisted other designers on many prestigious productions in the UK and abroad. He has also worked for the Tussauds Group and Wilson Phylaktis Architects.

Michael Spencer
Michael Spencer has been designing in the professional theatre for fifteen years since graduating from the Wimbledon School of Art in 1983. The range of his work incorporates community theatre, commercial tours, repertory theatre - featuring a long collaboration with director, Andrew Manley - and Opera. Highlights include an infamous *Marriage of Figaro* for Welsh National Opera in 1988 and three British premieres of David Mamet's adaptations of Chekhov plays: *The Cherry Orchard* (1989), *Uncle Vanya* (1990) and *The Three Sisters* (1996). In 1991 he returned to the Wimbledon School of Art to became the first person in this country to gain an MA in Theatre Design, which became the catalyst for a teaching career alongside the design commissions. He is currently Acting Course Director for the 'Theatre: Design for Performance' BA course at Central Saint Martins College of Art and Design in London. Recent work includes Euripides' *The Trojan Women* for the Cambridge Greek Play Society at the Cambridge Arts Theatre. Future design commissions include Tennessee William's *The Glass Menagerie* at the Wolsey Theatre, Ipswich.

Nancy Surman
Nancy Surman gained an honours degree in Theatre Design from Trent Polytechnic (now Nottingham Trent University) in 1988. Her first professional design was a production of *Shirley Valentine* at the Torch Theatre, Milford Haven. Since then she has worked extensively as a freelance designer, concentrating particularly on touring theatre. She designed the world premieres of *The Road to Hell* and *Johnny Watkins Walks on Water* (Birmingham Repertory Theatre); *The Magic Radio* (Byre Theatre, St Andrews); *A Stinging Sea* (Glasgow Citizens Theatre); and *Merlin's Return* (Torch Theatre). Other productions include *Kaahini* and *Bonded* (Birmingham Repertory Theatre); new adaptations of *Pride and Prejudice, Tom Jones, Far from the Madding Crowd* and *Maurice* (SNAP Theatre Company); *Squealing Like a Pig* and *Don Quixote* (Oxfordshire Touring Theatre Company); *Frankie and Tommy, Master Harold and the Boys, Lovers, The Final Appearance of Miss Mamie Stuart* and *Stepping Out* (Torch Theatre); *Laurel and Hardy* (Cheltenham Everyman). Amongst other things Nancy has recently been involved in the design of a Fête Champêtre to celebrate the National Trust's centenary.

Kit Surrey
Kit Surrey trained at Wimbledon School of Art (Diploma A.D., Stage Design) graduating in 1968. He began his career as assistant designer at the Citizens' Theatre, Glasgow designing experimental production in the Close Studio Theatre. He then moved to London where he worked extensively on the fringe and also at the Open Air Theatre, Regents' Park (1969-1971). In 1972 he was appointed Head of Design at the Theatre Royal, York and in 1974 Head of Design at the Northcott Theatre, Exeter. In 1976 he became freelance, working both in this country and abroad, and began a design relationship with the Royal Shakespeare company. Over the next 13 years he designed some 17 productions for the RSC ranging from main house productions for Stratford and the Barbican to the work of new writers at The Other Place (Stratford), The Warehouse and The Pit (London). He was appointed Associate Designer for The Warehouse (1979) and Associate Designer for Theatr Clwyd (also 1979). He represented Great Britain for the Scenographic Commission of the OISTAT in Moscow (1981) and Berlin (1982). He is also an established artist and was selected for the 1991 International Drawing Biennale and the 1993 Royal Academy Summer Exhibition as well as many galleries in the West Country where he has lived since 1974.

Ian Teague
Ian Teague trained at Trent Polytechnic (now Nottingham Trent University). He started work in 1982 as assistant designer at Liverpool Everyman. His design projects include main house repertory shows, community plays, small scale touring, TiE, YPT, youth theatre and college productions; in total over 90 productions. In 1997 he was commissioned by Amnesty International to design a large sculpture for use at music festivals and rallies. The majority of his work in recent years has been in the areas of TiE, YPT and community theatre. This has included productions for Oxfordshire Touring, Nuffield Theatre Southampton, Polka Children's Theatre, Arc Theatre Ensemble, Gazebo and Y Touring. His main interests have been in devising, new writing and developing a collaborative design process. Working with such companies as Tiebreak, Breakout, Gwent and most notably GYPT he has developed a range of devising and workshop skills and working practices (including the use of active research in schools). In addition to developing his process as a devisor this experience has informed his designing of extant texts. He has integrated devising methods into the rehearsal process. This has enabled him to create a richer more open and collaborative design process. He has been a member of British Actors' Equity Designers Committee since 1990. If you have access to the Internet you can see more of his work on his web site which can be found at: http://www.geocities.com/Broadway/Balcony/1816/.

Sophie Tyrrell
Sophie Tyrrell originally trained in Fine Art as a painter before studying Theatre Design at the University of Central England in Birmingham where she won the Sir Barry Jackson Award in her final year (1995). She went on to be shortlisted for the Linbury Prize for Stage Design that year. Opera designs include: Carlisle Floyd's *Susannah* (Midland Arts Centre); Tchaikovsky's *Eugene Onegin* (Birmingham Conservatoire); Mozart's *The Magic Flute* (Camden Opera); and Joseph Tahl's *The Garden* (Thameside Opera at the Queen Elizabeth Hall). She has worked on community and education projects for Opera North, Welsh National Opera, BBC Philharmonic Orchestra and Manchester Arts Education Festival. She has also designed productions for Contact Youth Theatre and various university companies.

Jamie Vartan
Jamie Vartan trained at the Central School of Art & Design, London. In 1988 he was awarded an Arts Council Theatre Designer's Bursary to Nottingham Playhouse. He has been working and travelling throughout 1998 as Designer/Artist in Residence for The David Glass Ensemble on *The Hansel Gretel Machine* (part one of *The Lost Child Trilogy*), which has included residencies involving workshops, research and performances in Vietnam, the Philippines, Colombia, China and Hong Kong as well as new productions devised with children in each country. This will continue in 1999 with *The Lost Child* (part two of the trilogy). Other design work for theatre includes: *Sour Grapes, The Hostage, A Little Like Paradise* and *The Playboy of the Western World* (Abbey Theatre, Dublin); *The House of the Spirits* (Tramway, Glasgow and West Yorkshire Playhouse); *Making History* (Teatro Tordinona, Rome); *Beau Jest* (Birmingham Old Rep and Bloomsbury Theatre, London); *Thorsilve* (Theatre Femina, Bordeaux); and *Off The Wall* (Polka Theatre for Children). Also several productions at Nottingham Playhouse. In opera, designs for *The Dwarf* (Teatro Comunale, Florence); *Aida* (Mid Wales Opera), *La Calisto* (Guildhall): *Cosi fan Tutte, Rigoletto, Don Giovanni* and *The Tales of Hoffmann* (Stowe Opera); *King Stag* and *Cat Man's Tale* (Opera Circus). Design for film includes: *Paradise Fish Bar* (BBC); *Smell* (Munich and Angers Film Festival Awards) and art director for *The King of Jazz* (BBC).

Janet Vaughan
Janet Vaughan trained at Nottingham Polytechnic and was the Belgrade Theatre in Education Company's Resident Designer from 1993 until its closure in the spring of 1996. As a freelancer, she has designed for site-specific and touring theatre as well as film works. She has also created artworks for non-gallery and outdoor spaces. Janet is closely associated with several of the Coventry Theatre Network's member companies and much of her theatre design work is made for devised productions or new writing originating in Coventry. With *Talking Birds*, Janet has designed all touring and site-specific theatre and film works over the last two years and in collaboration with composer/director Derek Nisbet she devised, designed and produced Recent Past, a multi-screen video installation with live piano trio, which premiered at the Adrian Boult Hall in Birmingham in 1998. Recent theatre design credits include: *Smoke, Mirrors and the Art of Escapology, Hotel 104* and *New Voyages in Suspense (Talking Birds)*; *Looking for the Tallyman* (Triangle); *Echoes and Omens* (Bare Essentials); *Wondrous Stories* (Theatre Absolute); *A Place of Refuge* (Big Brum); *Drink The Mercury* (Belgrade Theatre); *In Transit* (Motionhouse Dance Theatre); and *Past Caring* (Birmingham Rep and Fountain Theatre). Film design credits include: *Recent Past*, with live piano trio (Talking Birds with London Musici); *Ballistic Separation* (Talking Birds with Central TV); *2 Letters* (Talking Birds with London Musici, staged with live orchestra at the Queen Elizabeth Hall); and *Joy-ridden* (Maverick TV with Talking Birds).

Adrian Vaux
Adrian Vaux studied design at the Slade School. He was Resident Designer at London's Mermaid Theatre 1964-1970, Resident Designer at Leicester Phoenix and subsequently at the Haymarket, 1971-1980. He designed many productions during this time, some of which transferred to the West End, including *My Fair Lady, Cause Célèbre* and *Tomfoolery*. He was also Resident Designer at the London Old Vic 1980-1982. He began working in Israel in 1968 designing productions for Habimah, Cameri, Haifa and Jerusalem theatres. His association with Sobol began with original productions of *Weininger's Night, Ghetto, Palestinian Girl, Adam, Jerusalem Syndrome* and *Nice Toni*. This association led to working in Germany and the United States. Many of these productions raised highly controversial issues, both political and social such as the 'great silence' surrounding discussions of the Holocaust and the Israeli-Palestinian conflict.

Chris Victory
Chris Victory came into professional theatre some 5-6 years ago, having spent most of his life, from the age of 17, acting or directing in Gibraltar. He trained as a designer at Wimbledon School of Art and attained a first class honours degree in Theatre Design. Since then he has assisted on designs by James Hendy and Charles Edwards for opera companies such as D'Oyly Carte and Opera North before embarking on his own design career. Designs include: *Macbeth* and *The Taming of the Shrew* directed by Peter Benedict and Jenny Lee for Dreamakers at Wimbledon Theatre. For the last two years he has been working with Theatre Melange on its highly successful tours of *The Love of the Nightingale, The Hippolytos* and the new translation of Giradoux's *Ondine* by Steve Gooch, which was commissioned for Theatre Melange and received its world premiere in 1998.

Fiona Watt
Fiona Watt trained at Motley. She has an ongoing commitment to new writing. This has included work at the Tricycle alongside writers Bonnie Greer, Diane Samuels and Jenny McLeod creating new work with groups of young people, and developmental work with the Writers Laboratory programme at Paines Plough (1994-95). The lab 'buddied' writers with directors and designers throughout the writing process culminating in 'Writes of Spring', a showcase of three new plays. In 1996 Fiona was awarded an Arts Council design bursary to work at the Wolsey Theatre, Ipswich. This was a year-long residency designing across

the spectrum of main house, studio, regional touring and TiE. Recent credits include: *Heritage* by Nicola McCartney, directed by Philip Howard (Traverse Theatre, Edinburgh); *Outward Bound* by Sutton Vane, directed by Giles Croft (Palace Theatre, Watford); *No Name* by Wilkie Collins, directed by Ivan Cutting (Eastern Angles regional tour); *The Changelings* by Greg Cullen, directed by Tim Baker (Theatr Clwyd schools tour). Fiona was also designer for the film *Nitrate Won't Wait* (STV/Scottish Film Council First Reels). She is a member of the Designers Formation.

Karen Frances Webber

Karen Frances Webber trained at Nottingham Trent University and graduated with honours in 1996. Since 1997 she has worked as costume designer and deputy wardrobe supervisor for the Guildford School of Acting. Work there includes: *Chamber Music* (The Mill Studio, Guildford); *Cloud Nine, What About Leonardo?, Dick Whittington* and *Wondercat, Nine, Joan of Arc, Lady Chill* and *Children of Eden* (Bellairs Playhouse, Guildford); *Elegies, A Doll's House, A Chorus of Disapproval* and *The Caucasian Chalk Circle* (Electric Theatre, Guildford). Freelance work includes set and costume design for: *Through the Shadows* and *Broken Angel* (Yorkshire Women Theatre). Most recently she has designed costumes for the Zurich Insurance Corporate customer symposium in Lucerne based on the theme 'Looking back at the future'.

Ian Westbrook

Ian Westbrook trained in Theatre Design at Nottingham University. His first of many productions was with the Lenny Henry and Cannon and Ball shows for the Lord Delfont Group. After seasons at Nottingham, Leicester and Plymouth, he arrived in Norwich and began a long association with the Theatre Royal. He formed 3D Creations, a successful scenic design and construction company, based in workshops and studios near Great Yarmouth. Since then, his work has been seen in New York, Amsterdam, Vancouver, Berlin, Paris, London's West End and throughout the United Kingdom. In recent years, Ian's projects have included the *Holkham Hall Pageant* for the Earl of Leicester; the creation of a *Serengeti Safari Trail* for Her Majesty Queen Elizabeth II at Sandringham, *Sweeny Todd, The King and I, Brighton Rock, Great Expectations, Joseph and his Amazing Technicolor Dreamcoat, Cabaret* and *Fire from Heaven*, the Norwich Theatre Royal's Cathedral 900 Pageant. More recently, Ian was responsible for set painting on the world premiere of William Alwyn's opera *Miss Julie* also at the Theatre Royal Norwich. His designs have been seen in numerous Christmas shows across Britain including *Aladdin, Peter Pan, Jack and the Beanstalk, Cinderella* and *Babes in the Wood*. Ian has designed and created a large spaceship for a national theatre tour, designed the Oil of Ulay commercial promotion for German television and completed his fifth, and largest, Royal Commission for Her Majesty the Queen at Sandringham.

Bryan Williams

Bryan Williams began his career in retail display and design management for the John Lewis Partnership. Subsequently he returned to his heartland in the north of England where he co-established the award winning Northern Theatre Company which is now in its 24th year. Returning to an academic life as a mature student, Bryan studied Three Dimensional Design at Humberside University. Both during his studies and subsequent to graduation Bryan has created and supervised the construction of over 50 theatrical sets for his and other theatre companies such as Hull Truck. Much of this work was for original scripts, requiring him to become involved with the authors and directors at the earliest moments of the creative process, often before a word was written. Bryan also devotes part of his time to lecturing in higher education to help young designers get a start in their careers and a number of his former students now actually work in theatre and television.

Sarah Williamson

Sarah Williamson graduated from Central Saint Martins College of Art and Design in 1993. Between 1994 and 1996 she became Associate Designer and Acting Head of Design at the New Victoria Theatre in Stoke-on-Trent where she designed *Macbeth, Hansel and Gretel, Dear Nobody* and *Bedroom Farce*. She has since designed *The Merchant of Venice* (Royal Lyceum Theatre, Edinburgh), *Disappearances* (Salisbury Playhouse), *Far from the Madding Crowd* (Northcott Theatre, Exeter), *Taking Sides* (Library Theatre, Manchester), *Electra* (Cambridge Arts Theatre), *The Greatest Hits of British Theatre* and *The Football Factory* (Brighton Theatre Events, touring) and *Cavalleria Rusticana* and *I Pagliacci* (Opera Holland Park. Sarah also does a lot of educational work as a part-time and visiting lecturer at Brighton College of Technology and Central Saint Martins respectively and has led independent workshops and residencies with various schools and community groups.

Louise Ann Wilson

Louise Ann Wilson graduated from Nottingham Trent University in 1993 with a first class BA in Theatre Design. In the same year she exhibited *Mail Order Bride*, directed by Jude Kelly, for the Linbury Prize for Stage Design exhibition. Louise is co-artistic director of WilsonWilson Company formed in 1997 with director Wils Wilson; this company produces site-specific collaborative theatre with artists from different disciplines. The first piece of work, *House*, a collaboration with poet Simon Armitage, was a site-specific project created for a nineteenth century worker's cottage in Huddersfield. Future plans include a contemporary version of the Medea myth to be staged in diverse areas of a major city in Britain. Recent design work includes: *Some Voices* by Joe Penhall (Live Theatre); *Of Mice and Men*, an adaptation of Steinbeck's novel (touring venues ranging from a cattle market to country parks) won the Manchester Evening News Theatre Award for Best Special Event in 1997; *Three Girls in Blue* by Ludmilla Petrushevskaya (White Bear, Kennington) all directed by Wils Wilson. Louise has also designed for the West Yorkshire Playhouse Schools Company; the Sherman Theatre, Cardiff, the Gate, Notting Hill, Theatre Centre, Meeting Ground and numerous site-specific productions including *Rites Rules Wrongs* in the Park Tunnel, Nottingham.

Andrew Wood

Andrew Wood studied theatre at Nottingham Trent Polytechnic and graduated in 1991. He worked as a freelance designer before joining Contact Theatre in Manchester where he filled every position in the design department from assistant through to Head of Design to Associate Director (Design) between 1993 and 1998. Designs for Contact include: *Romeo and Juliet, Speed-the-Plow, The Trial* and the touring production of *The Mill on the Floss*. Other work for Contact includes their last six Young Playwright

Festivals and within the Theatre Lab Outsider Project. Recent freelancing includes: *Neville's Island* and *Blithe Spirit* (Harrogate Theatre); *Future Tense Festival* for New Writing North; and as a visiting lecturer at the Liverpool Institute for Performing Arts, Manchester, Manchester Metropolitan and Salford Universities.

Haibo Yu

Haibo Yu trained as a theatre designer at the Central Academy of Drama in China where he executed a number of designs for theatre and television productions. He obtained a scholarship to study at the University of Leeds in 1986 and then transferred to a post graduate course at Central Saint Martins College of Art and Design in London. His designs have been widely seen in theatre, film and television. Among his recent works are included films: *Foreign Moon* (Media Asia, Hong Kong), *The Opium War* (UK locations, Xie Jin Films, Shanghai); television: *The Historic Turning Point* (Transatlantic Films, London); and theatre designs: *Bright Angel, Babble* (Proteus Theatre Company, southern tour); and *Whale* (Harrogate Theatre). He is currently teaching design at St. Mary's University College and has designed 50 productions in the college theatre and studio.

index of productions

Theatre Spaces

Research Project

Installations

index of companies

index of designers

Martin Johns 60
Mark Jonathan 73, 106
Paul W Jones 20
Robert Jones 83
Sophie Jump 110

Michael Keegan-Dolan 58
Vic Kilpatrick 69
Ed King 110
Thornsten Knaub 109
Spyros D Koskinas 97

Anthony Lamble 12
Jason Larcombe 48
Stefanos Lazaridis 94, 95, 100, 101
John Leberg 54
Marie-Jeanne Lecca 88, 94, 95, 100, 101
Brent Lees 40
Fiona Lewry 58, 65, 74
Robin Linklater 59
Keith Lodwick 28
Lurca 107
Claire Lyth 74

Tina MacHugh 30
Nick MacLiammoir 80
Ian MacNeil 102
Tanya McCallin 58
Gary McCann 67
Charlotte McClelland 21
Peter McKintosh 30, 46
Tom Mannings 23
Fred Marchal 47
Christine Marfleet 43
Nick Marston 15, 18
David Martin 40
Diane Martin 52
Jocelyn Meall 74
Fred Meller 29, 73
Lucinda Meredith 8
Madeleine Millar 47
Simon Mills 71
Clare Mitchell 102
Richard Moffet 109
Brian Moorhouse 9
Martin Morley 76
Nicola Morton 98
Muir 107
Peter Mumford 25, 93, 104
Ruari Murchison 106
Neil Murray 30, 31

Daniele Naldi 62
Dody Nash 47
Pippa Nissen 14

Paul O'Neill 67
Jim O'Reilly 40
Christopher Oram 32
Giuseppe di Orio 88
Kate Owen 80

Gregoris Papageorgiou 19
Mark Passey 73
Rob Pepper 28
Celia Perkins 29, 48
Andy Phillips 33
Tom Phillips 8
Dana Pinto 98
Christine Piper 82
Tom Piper 34, 35
Michael Poyner 63

Jason Redgrave 48
Christopher Richardson 79
Nick Richings 55
Richard Riddell 8
Renny Robertson 98
Isabel Robson 49
Marise Rose 40
Felice Ross 36
Cathy Ryan 77

Paul Sadot 108
Emma Sainsbury 108
Alan Schofield 51
Nettie Scriven 77
Jan P Sendor 114, 115
Keith Shanks 63
Nick Sharton 38
Paul Sheard 118
Juliet Shillingford 78
Georgina Shorter 50
Tim Skelly 60
Kevin Sleep 12, 26, 74
Joanne Smith 85
Edna Sobol 36
Ian Sommerville 22, 35, 117
Paul Sorley 8
George Souglides 88
Michael Spencer 38
Stuart Stocks 38
Nancy Surman 57
Kit Surrey 96
Sandro Sussi 84

Simon Tapping 55
Jason Taylor 26
Julie Taymor 45
Ian Teague 75
Ian Townsend 60
Bryan Tweddle 40
Sophie Tyrrell 23

Hugh Vanstone 64
Jamie Vartan 37
Janet Vaughan 99
Adrian Vaux 36
Chris Victory 12

Julie Washington 29
Fiona Watt 98
Karen Frances Webber 80
Ian Westbrook 52
Bruce J Williams 50
Bryan Williams 96
Sarah Williamson 32, 33
Louise Ann Wilson 79
Andrew Wood 92

Kamilla Yakubova 49
Haibo Yu 118

**Theatre Architects
and Consultants**

Ian Albery : Theatre Consultant
for Sadler's Wells Trust Ltd. 113
Arts Team @ RHWL 113
Austin-Smith:Lord 10
Carr and Angier 10
MEB Partnership Architects 79
Theatre Futures 79

timespace

design for performance 1995 - 1999

ENTERTAINMENTS